A Cheerful Ascetic

and

Other Essays

A CHEERFUL ASCETIC

AND

OTHER ESSAYS

By

JAMES J. DALY, S.J.

Professor of English
University of Detroit

THE BRUCE PUBLISHING COMPANY

NEW YORK   MILWAUKEE   CHICAGO

PREFACE BY THE GENERAL EDITOR

There has long been a demand for publication in book form of the literary work of Father James J. Daly, S.J. His essays, wherever they appear, are invariably welcomed with pleasure and keen appreciation by a wide circle of readers. The artistry of his style; the winsome yet profound spirituality of his thought, which never loses hold of human interest; the delicate nuances of his wit; the play of light and shadow that passes over his pages like the clouds and rippling wind over a sunlit field; the freedom of Catholic expression, frank with the candor of a child, yet never offensive to those without the Fold, should cast a spell over all who will come into contact with the author.

The present volume, the editor hopes, is but the harbinger of others to come. He is especially grateful for the kindly coöperation of the Editors of the *Month*, the *Catholic World*, the *Queen's Work*, *Thought*, and *America*.*

Joseph Husslein, S.J., Ph.D.,
General Editor, Science and Culture Series.

---

*Reprinted with permission from the *Month* (London): "A Cheerful Ascetic," "Some Letters of Joyce Kilmer"; *Thought:* "Charles Waterton: Naturalist"; the *Catholic World:* "Sir Thomas More: Saint and Humorist," "Sir Thomas More: The Spiritual Writer," "The Paganism of Mr. Yeats," "A Poet of Our Lady"; *America:* "The Intolerant Emerson"; the *Queen's Work:* "Sir Thomas More: The Happy Warrior," "Religion and a Career: Sir John Day," "Religion and a Career: Lord Charles Russell."

CONTENTS

A CHEERFUL ASCETIC

IT will be remembered that, when Alexander the Great asked Diogenes what he could do for him, the philosopher requested that the king might be pleased to step aside out of his light. This story has always made me feel kindly toward Alexander. Renunciation ceases to be admirable when it plants itself on the heights of self-conscious superiority. Just so, I cannot enter into Emerson's enthusiasm over the famous reply of his friend Thoreau, who, when asked what was his favorite dish, answered, "The nearest." He scorned the rest of us poor dogs. Crates, and all cynical philosophers of ancient and modern times, run as true to paganism as any Epicurean. There is an orgy of pride as well as of the senses; the former is probably the more deadly of the two. *"Aude, hospes, contemnere opes,"* Evander exhorted Æneas; and the reward promised for greatly daring to despise wealth was association with the gods, in Olympian aloofness from mere human herds.

It is not hard or heroic to flout Fortune if thereby we nourish our self-esteem. As long as we think we are fine porcelain in a world of clay, what matters it whether we live in a tub, or a kennel, or a shanty by Walden pond, or a marble palace. Marcus Aurelius and his successors kept assiduous diaries, and drew isothermic maps of

1

their mental state every day, and compiled weather reports out of them for the guidance of the less wise. Each thought his observatory the holiest temple in the universe and cut a gallant figure before admirers by flinging a scornful glove in the face of Fortune. They were rough to her when they thought anyone was looking. We now suspect that they courted her in secret.

When pride completes the circle of humility the two extremes meet on a common ground of asceticism. This juxtaposition in one and the same setting has deceived many. It is a strange fact that sanctity and sin should at times in their supreme human forms issue in contempt for the lower pleasures. Experts have the hardest work sometimes to determine which is which. One cannot always judge infallibly even in his own case. It is sometimes beyond all but the highest capacity "to disentangle the threads of a proud self-respect from the purely Christian texture" in the complex web of motives which make up one's spiritual life. A clever person might be expected to be able to detect the considerable difference between God and himself. But it is precisely the clever persons who are always getting themselves confused about two objects which clearly ought to be far more distinguishable apart than a hawk from a handsaw.

I do not pretend to the power of laying down rules in the matter. If I were to hazard an opinion, it would be that the true asceticism of noble spirits is never armored either with prickly eccentricities or starched coats of respectability or forbidding displays of individualism and temperament. It rather believes in and practices disarmament, and exposes itself, after a manner resembling a merry invitation, to every approach, whether friendly or hostile. It calls for the exercise of coldest nerve, most deliberate courage, unquailing endurance, and judgment balanced to the nicety of a hair. None of the brave valors of war, adventure, or love, make so many demands upon ingenuity and swift decision. Listen to the story of Francis de Cardona and judge whether I speak the truth.

Francis was the son of a Spanish duke.[1] I have taken the incidents in his life, which I am about to relate, from Louis de Ponte's classic biography of Balthasar Alvarez. The son of the Duke of Cardona was Rector of the University of Salamanca when he took it into his head to spurn the rich pledges of fortune by entering a Jesuit novitiate. One of his first charges was the care of the community refectory. Do not entertain the picture of a *maître d'hôtel* in evening clothes, by a glance maintaining order in the scurrying lines of communication between the kitchen and the trenchermen. It was the business of Francis to scrub floors and to wash dishes with as little damage as possible. His distinguished friend, Dr. Oiedo, found him so employed and was shocked and scandalized. The ex-Rector of the Uni-

---

[1]De Ponte calls him Francis of Cardona, son of the Duke of Cardona and Segorva, Marquis of Comares, but does not tell us how he had come to occupy the important post of Rector of a University wherein he was later on to become a student.

versity was genuinely bewildered at the good doctor's strange point of view. He declared that he was having the time of his life and would not exchange his job for that of the Pope himself, and sent his visitor away thinking so furiously that he too plunged into the same adventure and followed Francis into the novitiate.

It was not long before Cardona made the interesting discovery that life, no matter how we arrange it, is sure to have its puzzles and perplexities. "The thread of life, like other threads or skeins of silks, is full of snarls and incumbrances." Francis had made a bonfire of his riches and honors, and set out without impediments upon a spiritual quest. He thought he had succeeded in simplifying life, and was astonished to find he had only made its complexities more subtle and insidious. When Fortune ceases to be pursued she becomes the pursuer; she refuses to be ignored. Francis had failed to understand that menial services in the scullery assume the character of brilliant performances when a Spanish grandee and ex-Rector of a University undertakes them. He found himself moving in an aura of admiration. Superiors and brethren were highly edified by his humility. Horrors! Canonization is necessarily a post-mortem affair; else it is a menace and an infernal nuisance. Francis found himself in a painful dilemma. He sat down to ponder on the curious fact that there is a limit beyond which one may not go in flouting Fortune, without falling into the opposite extreme of the most ingratiating courtship of her; as Cicero's philosophers became famous by writing books in contempt of fame.

A less resourceful character than Francis would have crawled back into his shell and followed a policy of caution which would have robbed the world of much exquisite delight. He yearned for the mad excitement of trailing Fortune's banners in the mire: at the same time, he must, above all things, elude the applause of sharp-eyed and discerning associates. This was the task which Francis de Cardona set himself: his life henceforth resolved itself largely into a series of brave and amusingly clever attempts to accomplish it. "What I shall say may be unhesitatingly believed," writes de Ponte in introducing his account of Francis, citing as his authority Francis's contemporary and friend, Father Oiedo, "whose virtues are a guarantee of his sincerity." Three centuries have done nothing to blur the picture which still preserves the freshness of life, a delicious mixture of quizzical humor, high spirits, stern and unfaltering purpose, and spiritual exaltation sweetly and humanly attractive.

In every large establishment there are two places where the exercise of patience, unsupported by any approving recognition, is in special demand; the kitchen and the stable. Francis was not long in a Jesuit house before he fixed his attention upon these two precincts as very promising fields for the plying of his little private business. He prepared the way by confidential disclosures of certain weaknesses of his to everyone in the house, "You know, I have always had an intense interest in the cuisine and the stud. I take the liberty of considering myself an accomplished amateur in both departments. You should see some of my dishes! It is a crying shame that idle gourmets should enjoy all the good things for themselves. Are the servants of God never to be refreshed according to their due when they are worn out by study and prayer and the labors of the ministry? Ah, if I could only tinker and potter about at large in the kitchen and watch my favorite pudding swell into a brown miracle! Trust me to do pigeon to a turn. And as for horses, carissime, I dote on horses. How they must miss me! Carissime, if I were not a Jesuit, I think I should be either a cook or a Gitano." In such guileful wise did Francis proceed. Now, Jesuits, who figure in the world's legends as crafty beings, can furnish, as Francis observed, an astonishing amount of simplicity to practice upon. While there is evidence of vague doubts and films of incredulity, owing perhaps to the jealousy of the regular cook and the established stablehands, and perhaps also to some rather glaring failures of Francis in his chosen employments, still the rank and file of the community could not come to a conclusion. After all, noblemen, we know, cultivate surprising eccentricities. This is an amiable weakness of Francis, our brother, a survival of his masterful past. Let him indulge it if he enjoys it.

"The care of animals," says de Ponte, "was a task he sought after, and in which he said he was very skilful.

The superior did not believe it, of course; but he willingly gave him this commission to please him. This gave rise to a very edifying incident." Before we proceed to narrate this incident let us pause to salute that superior. Francis thought he was having all the fun. But Father Superior was not so simple as he looked when he gave this Spanish grandee head in his mad career through the china shops of convention, not altogether hopeless of getting some amusement, and inconvenience perhaps, out of the thing himself. Father Superior was a shrewder man than his Father Minister, as we shall see.

One day a Father from a remote province arrived at the Jesuit house in Salamanca, mounted on a sorry nag in the last stages of emaciation and exhaustion. The poor beast was covered with sores and could scarcely maintain an upright position. A little group had formed around the animal in the courtyard, trying to interpret, as charitably as might be, the visitor's choice of a mount. Francis happened along at the time and with the swift intuition of genius recognized a golden opportunity. "Father Minister," he said, "I think I can save that horse which seems to be in a bad way." It would look as if Father Minister, who is the one that manages details of the house, had reason to suspect the expert qualifications of Francis. But, according to the account of Father de Ponte, Francis urged his point with so much eloquence that, after hemming and hawing and many a dubious regard, Father Minister finally yielded a reluctant consent. It is hard to see why the good Father hesitated over the simple request unless he had some mysterious premonition of what was to follow.

Now began a very saturnalia, so to speak, of humiliation. The situation, as it unfolded, developed rich possibilities. It turned out to be even a more excellent opportunity than Francis had anticipated, and I think we shall all agree that he rose to it perfectly. He first dressed all the equine sores and then applied bandages of brilliant and varied colors. It was observed—for Father Minister was reconnoitering uneasily on the outskirts—it was observed that after everything was ready for the trip to the pasture at the other end of Salamanca, Francis wasted some time in an absorbing study of the position of the sun in the heavens. "What nonsense," growled Father Minister under his breath, "as if the conjunction of the planets could cure a horse!" At last the right astrological moment seemed to arrive, and Francis started off down the main avenue of the city. It took him by the principal entrance of the University, then in the heyday of its prosperity, not dreaming of its sad spoliation in the Napoleonic wars. Francis had studied the position of the sun to a nicety. He reached the gates of the University just as the students were swarming out by hundreds. Delectable sight! Ex-Rector and Spanish nobleman, with a cast-off cap on his head and a stableman's cloak slung about him, leading by a halter down the most crowded thoroughfare of Salamanca the gorgeously bandaged and limping remains of an ancient steed in the last stages of dissolution! A mob of jeering and appreciative urchins furnished the complement of the quaint parade. History stops to note that there was "something of an air of triumph in his countenance." Of course! How sudden and splendid opportunity can be! That morning, when the clamorous bell had tumbled him out of his narrow cot in the dormitory, the opening eye of day was dull and sleepy, without the remotest hint of what was coming. And now here he was wallowing, so to speak, in the heartiest repudiation of the nice respectabilities and punctilios of Fortune. He had her bound hand and foot, and was dragging her at his chariot wheels, or rather at the heels of his borrowed and wobbling Rosinante, down all the gutters of Salamanca. "Something of an air of triumph on his countenance," quotha!

We are told that after the first flurry of sensation had swept over the gaping crowds, "some praised, some blamed and many just laughed at it." Among those who blamed were certain sensitive young Jesuits who were among the throngs pouring out of the lecture rooms in time to behold the spectacle which their brother Francis had staged. They were chagrined beyond measure that the Jesuits should thus be exposed to the mockery of the city by the ill-regulated piety of a silly novice. They could scarcely get home in time to report the matter to the Superior. They burst in on him precipitately and stated their grievance. He entered into their point of view, sympathized with them in this common disgrace, and dismissed them with the assurance that the thing would be looked into. After they had gone, the Superior, we may suppose, enjoyed a quiet chuckle. That evening he called Francis upon the carpet. Could not Francis humiliate himself without humiliating the whole house? It was an act of charity and lowlihood to befriend the crippled beast, but why had he not made a detour through the side street to the suburb where the paddock lay? Must he choose the most frequented street and busiest hour for the performance of a menial service, to the great pain and confusion of his brethren? Francis expressed concern and repentance for causing his brothers pain and laid the blame on his incorrigible indolence which was always choosing the shortest and easiest road. When the door had closed on this interview, we may again suppose that Father Superior enjoyed his second chuckle that day. All the same, he summoned Father Minister and warned that poor distracted man to be wary with his permissions to carissimus Francis.

The query naturally suggests itself whether Francis may not have been an unbalanced and eager pietist to whom any extravagance was likely to recommend itself as a logical expression of spiritual convictions. That he was the son of a Duke is a circumstance which throws no light on the matter. It is harder to reconcile such a supposition with the fact that as a young man he had been chosen to fill the office of Rector in Spain's principal university. Francis would have welcomed with ravishment any general impression that he was below mediocrity in strong-mindedness and intelligence. It grieved him that the large outstanding fact of his former rectorship would effectually prevent the wide currency of such a belief. Here was another nut to be cracked. How our past haunts us! We cannot outlive even our honors. We have to confess that, in devising a plan to destroy his domestic reputation for scholarship and sound sense, Francis did not play up quite to his usual standard of ingenuity. Still, it has to be admitted, he raked in larger results than one might expect from a somewhat clumsy experiment.

One day he was delivering, as is the custom, a sermon in the refectory while the community was eating dinner. It is an excellent exercise, in homiletics for the novice-preacher, in other things for the community. It was the panegyric of a saint, and in discussing a controverted point in the saint's biography Francis made the following remarkable statement: "I have consulted two editions of the *Flos Sanctorum* and I find they do not agree; but, if I must give my opinion, I adopt the text of the Augsburg edition, because the type is clearer and easier to read." A shout of laughter went up from the tables to the annoyance of Father Minister, while Francis waited in a composure of mournful gravity for the hilarity to simmer down. He knew he had been clumsy. But, unskilfully as he had cast his net, it was not wholly empty when he drew it home. Listen to the words of de Ponte in which humor and piety struggle for ascendancy. "One of them," he says, "actually believed that Francis was serious, through the permission of Divine Providence, in order to carry out the humble intention of His servant." The biographer felt that Providence had to be introduced, like a *deus ex machina,* before his readers would believe that one member of the community could be deceived by such a transparent artifice. De Ponte tells us more about this slow-witted person. "Persuaded that the holy man was a simpleton, he not only laughed at this incident, but continued to make game of him on all occasions, and even in his presence." Francis was overjoyed. He fastened himself to this novice, sought his company, performed friendly offices for him, showered him with attentions, chose him for partner in their daily walks. And all the time the goose of a novice was treating Francis as an idiot, ordering him about and ridiculing him to such an extent that he became known as the "persecutor" of Francis. That Francis was not drawing him on for the foolery of the thing is clear from the upshot. One of the minor officials of the house—not Father Superior, we may be sure—called Francis to explain his constant attendance on this misguided novice. Particular friendships and coteries can break up the best-regulated families and states, and are to be guarded against in religious communities. Francis tried evasions; but his inquisitor was ruthless. He was driven into a corner and pinned down. "Your reverence and my brethren," explained Francis at last in much disgust,

"treat me honorably, as if I were somebody, which is
no advantage to me. This man alone knows me, and
does me justice by laughing at me and turning to ridi-
cule whatever I do and say. Since this good Brother
labors thus for my interest, is it not natural that I
should prefer his company to that of others?"

When Aquinas was asked how to become a great saint,
he is reported to have said: "Will it." Now, while we
do not like to differ from a saint on the subject of
sanctity, we respectfully urge the experience of Francis
de Cardona in support of the theory that it is not merely a question of good will. Unless, of course, sanctity
presupposes intelligence of such a high order that native
resourcefulness reduces every difficulty to a bagatelle.
If the worst befalls, and the saint is caught, as we say,
red-handed, he knows how to brazen it out. Sanctity,
like murder, will out. The vices and virtues probably
run equal chances of discovery. In either case disclosure
is embarrassing. The direful contingency does not act
as a check on the hardened criminal. The same seems to
be true of the hardened saint. Francis did much plung-
ing and wriggling and dodging before allowing himself
to be caught; but, when the game was up, he laughed
and started a new one.

We do not hear much of Francis during his years of
study, teaching, and active work in the ministry, except that he was everywhere popular. It is related that
he made a compact with one of his associates to meet at
certain stated times when each would inform the other

of faults he had noted in him. Francis, we may be sure, picked out a stern-eyed argus. After they had come together several times, and Francis had been liberally supplied with criticisms without contributing a single return in kind, the other man objected to the one-sided business. Francis could only reply that he was kept so busy with his own large and unruly family of faults that he really had no time to watch other people's. A magnanimous man, indeed!

At the end of a Jesuit's course of formation there is a third year of probation, called tertianship, resembling the first two years of novitiate, and occupied exclusively with the spiritual life. What with the breathless succession of lectures and "circles" during his studies, and the dignity which a teacher and preacher must preserve in the colleges and churches, Francis often looked forward to this year as to a paradise wherein he might riot with the respectabilities as in the good old days at Salamanca. The famous Father Alvarez was tertian-master, himself a gay trifler with the solemn usages of what Carlyle used to style gig-philosophy, a man after Francis's own heart. We come now to the last episode in the life of Francis, son of the Duke of Cardona and former Rector of the University of Salamanca. Everyone will agree that in his exit he acted up to his usual form.

A neighboring market town, the site of country fairs, afforded a fine field to the "Tertians" for getting rid of their self-respect. On fair-days the drovers and cattle dealers could enjoy or curse, as their humors and the turn of the market dictated, the presence, among the swarming beggars, of young Jesuits, the finished products of the schools, going about hat in hand soliciting alms. This was a splendid opening for Francis, who had nothing to do but find new ways of snubbing the world, the flesh, and the devil. He heard that the lay brother in charge of the farmyard contemplated buying some hogs at the fair. Forthwith he recalled that he was a connoisseur of hogs, and accordingly presented himself in the rôle before Father Alvarez, expressing great concern lest the simple brother, left to his own devices, should be swindled in the transaction. He humbly sought permission to accompany the brother as an expert. Father Alvarez assented with mock gravity and doubtless with wondering surmises regarding the event.

That was a gala day for Francis; as was fitting, since it was his last adventure. The fair-day crowds had the thrilling and unlooked-for pleasure of seeing a Spanish grandee serving as a swine-herd with tremendous earnestness. On the way home one of the little pigs went lame; and, in the words of our chronicler, "Father Francis took it up by the feet and put it on his shoulders in the position given to the sheep carried by the Good Shepherd." Grandeeism groaned that day in Spain, as this curious cortège moved across the landscape in a cloud of dust. When they reached home late in the evening, the brother suddenly became aware that, with culpable improvidence, he had forgotten to prepare lodging for these new additions to his livestock. There was nothing for Francis to do but to start in, late as was the hour and wearied by the unusual exertions of the day, to help the brother build a pig pen. Francis rode nature a little too hard on that red-letter day. Fever seized him in grim earnest, and carried him off in eleven days. When the last moment came and he was kicking the old earth from under, with its dukedoms and lord-rectorships and mincing respectabilities, it is probable, though history conveys no tidings here, that he heaved a sigh of relief over the near prospect of a place where the spirit could pursue happiness in simplified conditions, undistracted by the powerful and sinister cross-currents of time.

Thus went out for ever an intense little flame among those bright and daring spirits, who each in his own generation shine like sparks of fire in the reeds. I have said nothing of the ultimate motive behind all this prodigality of valor. That is a story by itself. Everyone can see that, whatever the motive, it must have been stronger than life or death.

CHARLES WATERTON: NATURALIST

O UR English literature, as we all know, has passed through its best growing years during an overwhelming Protestant ascendency. For several centuries there were so few Catholic writers that Englishmen might almost be excused for thinking that not only the iron and coal and wealth of old England, but its strong and beautiful language also, were the fitting rewards granted by a bountiful and appreciative Providence to approved national types of Christianity. When Lingard appeared, employing, strange to say, a remarkably pure and idiomatic English, his excellence seemed to be resented, as if he had no right to be as good as he was; and the less said about him, the better. There was an audible gasp of astonishment, accompanied by something like indignation, when Newman arose on a larger stage than Lingard's and proceeded to use the English language as a garment for Catholic thought. The fit was perfect. That the speech of Englishmen should be heard in a Catholic galley was bad enough; that it should seem to be at home there, as if nothing at all had happened in the interval between Sir Thomas More and the Duke of Cumberland, was a mystery and an outrage requiring time and patience to digest.

17

It is sometimes alleged that Catholics exaggerate the literary excellence of their own writers. The suspicion has been entertained that Patmore and Francis Thompson and Joyce Kilmer, for instances, are the pets of Catholic coteries and have been nursed into a largely factitious prominence. If this be so, the years will tell. But the suspicion seems unwarranted. The Catholic reading public has neither the numbers nor the influence to initiate popular literary estimates. If it tosses its cap in the air for a coreligionist, it is only after the cheers have been started elsewhere.

Nay, sometimes the cheering finds few or no echoes. Take Charles Waterton. His famous book, *Wanderings in South America,* appeared in 1825. It leaped into immediate popularity. Sydney Smith wrote a long review of it in his best manner for the *Edinburgh.* It was assailed by the stay-at-home naturalists—the "closet-naturalists" as Waterton ironically styled them—and provoked a controversy like that which raged during the consulship of Roosevelt around the so-called nature fakers. And since its appearance a century ago, it has never been allowed to gather dust in the limbo of the top shelf. The original publisher—not a Catholic publisher—issued a sixth edition about the time Waterton died. In 1878, the Rev. J. G. Wood, an Anglican clergyman and distinguished naturalist—he delivered the Lowell lectures in Boston in 1883—edited an edition of the *Wanderings* with a biographical introduction. This useful edition has been reprinted six times.

At least two American editions have appeared. In 1909, a New York publishing house (Sturgis and Walton) printed a handsome edition, with an introduction and illustrations by Charles Livingston Bull, and a memoir by Norman Moore, Waterton's biographer in the *Dictionary of National Biography*. The *Wanderings* is one of the latest additions in the "Everyman's Library" series of classics. It is curious to note that Newman and Waterton are the only two Catholic names in that series among the writers of the past hundred years. Not long ago the London *Times* devoted a large part of the leading article of its Literary Supplement to a consideration of Waterton, as the possessor of a permanent place in English literature. And about the same time, an English magazine of the popular kind printed some reminiscences, in which Sir Austen Chamberlain stated that the *Wanderings* was the favorite book of his boyhood. These are straws; but they would indicate that Waterton's work is still raising a little wind.

The element of strangeness about all this is the apparently resolute way in which Catholics have held aloof from all demonstrations in favor of Waterton. He published, besides the *Wanderings,* three volumes of natural-history essays, four volumes in all. Seldom can any one of the four be found in a Catholic library. No Catholic publisher's list contains a Waterton title. Two histories of English literature which have been consulted, both written by Catholics, omit all mention of Waterton. Whenever a reference is made to Waterton in a Catholic periodical, it is done in the manner of one airing his erudition, and is generally inaccurate.

There is so little conceivable reason for the neglect that it actually takes on the lineaments of a mystery. It cannot be because Waterton is a naturalist, and therefore writing outside the circle of common human interest. While he is a naturalist of eminence, he always had impatience, amounting to contempt, for the learned and cumbersome paraphernalia of scientific pedantry. Much to the dismay of the naturalists who recognize his high worth, he never attached the accepted Greek and Latin labels to the objects of his study. He used the popular names, and discussed nature in the large and easy way of a man of the world who knew a thing or two besides the matter in hand. He has far more of the human and the personal in his studies than Gilbert White. These are, after all, superfluous arguments on the side of a book like the *Wanderings,* which, as a matter of fact, is regarded even in the *Cambridge History of English Literature,* as a literary classic. If the book is interesting to the world at large, it ought to be sufficiently interesting to Catholic readers.

While a book of travels is always sure of a certain measure of welcome, it is perhaps right to surmise that it stands a better chance in a country like England than in a self-supporting country like our own. Every second person in England either has a relation beyond the seas, or looks forward to a colonial career. Although the government is alarmed over the declining interest in the colonial civil service among the undergraduates of Oxford and Cambridge, the names of Clive, Hastings, and Rhodes are still potent to stir youthful imaginations. We can understand why Waterton's book of travel should be more popular in England than in America. But we do not understand why it should be more popular among non-Catholic Englishmen than among Catholic Englishmen.

There are three kinds of Catholic writers. Those who find it impossible, from some limitation in their art or personality, to make literary material out of their religious experience; those who learn to play a discreet Catholic accompaniment in their literary entertainments; and finally those who are boisterously Catholic before any and every audience. If Waterton belonged to the first, or even the second of these three classes, Catholics might be excused for not paying him special attention. But this, in the language of the penny thriller, is just where the mystery deepens. Waterton is uproariously Catholic. He scorned concealments. In his clear and simple view of the matter, it was the other fellow, the child of the Reformation, who ought to practice concealments. He always blessed himself in public, figuratively speaking and probably literally speaking also, with the biggest and most deliberate sign of the cross that he could make. He waved the papal colors with a joyous delight in the face of early Victorian England, which was a very Protestant England indeed. How England came to swallow him, remains as great a mystery as how Catholics came to forget him.

The first of these two mysteries becomes less insoluble on a further acquaintance with Charles Waterton. He was a man of so much transparent honesty and goodness that his most objectionable enthusiasms wore a convincing air of unselfish idealism and chivalry. He was a friend of Thackeray, met him in Rome, and tried to convert him. We nearly all like Thackeray; but just think of anyone trying to make a Catholic out of that lovable worldling, with all his inherited insular prepossessions strong upon him! The attempt is described in the *Newcomes*, where the hero is writing home from Rome: that the ludicrous side of the incident is not played up as much as it might be, is evidence of goodness of heart in both men.

A friend, who belongs to the old religion, took me, last week, into a church where the Virgin lately appeared in person to a Jewish gentleman, flashed down upon him from heaven in light and splendor celestial, and of course, straightway converted him. My friend bade me look at the picture, and, kneeling down beside me, I know prayed with all his honest heart that the truth might shine down upon me too; but I saw no glimpse of heaven at all; all I saw was a poor picture, an altar with blinking candles, a church hung with tawdry strips of red and white calico. The good kind W. went away humbly saying "that such might have happened again if heaven so willed it." I could not but feel a kindness and admiration for the good man. I know his works are made to square with his faith, that he dines on a crust, lives as chastely as a hermit, and gives his all to the poor.

Alas, the spiritual dispositions of Thackeray were not precisely those of the Abbé Alphonse Ratisbon. If the simple and sanguine temper of Waterton were doomed to disappointment on this occasion, we can still regard the incident as one of the rarest and most touching things in history. It might have won mention in Hazlitt's "Of Persons One Would Wish To Have Seen," if that fine essay had been written some fifty years later.

When Waterton liked a man, he wanted to be sure of liking him for all eternity. Doctor Hobson—Richard Hobson, M. D. Cantab.—was his family physician and close friend. In the year following Waterton's death, Dr. Hobson published a garrulous book entitled: *Charles Waterton: His Home, Habits, and Handiwork. Reminiscences of an Intimate and Most Confiding Personal Association of Nearly Thirty Years.* It testifies to the popularity of Waterton, rather than to the skill of the memoirist, that the book ran into a second edition within five months of its first appearance. The doctor's affection and reverence for his friend are the most noticeable features of the large acreage of verbiage; but the reader's patience is sometimes rewarded. The doctor writes, referring to the apparition of our Lady and her shrine at La Salette, which Waterton had been visiting.

He, of course, on his return, largely expatiated on it, and insisted on my chiming in with him to the full extent of his own self-conviction. He was amazed how I could be so obtuse and bigoted as not to be at once proselytized, expressing the greatest surprise that I was so perverse and hoodwinked as not to go along with him even in his "tolerant belief." After earnestly expostulating with me, "I have," he observed, "often heard it said that none are so deaf as those who won't hear, but I can bear testimony that none are so blind as those who won't see." Although we were both emphatic in our disputation, yet our controversy was invariably maintained with such a thorough conviction of the sincerity of a sacred veneration for the cause we espoused that a word of anger never escaped the lips of either of us. I entertain not the shadow of a doubt but that the squire indulged to the fullest extent in the firm belief of the appearance of the apparition of the Blessed Virgin to the two shepherd children: and that no argument, however sound or lucidly expressed and convincing to Protestants, nor any amount of persuasive powers, however bewitchingly used, could have created an atom of doubt or disbelief in his mind.

The good doctor was a patient and cheerful Boswell. His stanch Protestant ears had to submit to eulogies of the "Romish Church," constantly pledged as the *caput mundi* against the Protestant *caput mortuum*. Nor was the squire without his patience, too. If the doctor obstinately refused to be saved, the zealous apostle, on the other hand, never allowed his temper to be affected. And this is a gentle courtesy not always achievable by zealous apostles.

Waterton, it must be admitted, had certain advantages in his public and private bullying of English prejudices. Much can be forgiven a man whose ancestors fought at Cressy and Agincourt and Marston Moor, and are mentioned by Shakespeare in his *Richard II*. Moreover, he was a landed proprietor and unquestionably belonged to the gentry. Such a man is sure of being allowed considerable leeway on the score of amiable eccentricities. It is extremely doubtful, however, whether the honest and fearless squire was aware of the indulgence his social position could command; but, whether or no, he never appeared nervous about over-straining it. He seized every opportunity of praising the Catholic Church and, in particular, the Jesuits. He always referred to the Reformers of the sixteenth century in terms of gross and most appalling disrespect. The only living thing he did not love and cherish was the rat, and he paid his respects to the reigning royal house by always calling a rat a "Hanoverian rat," because it "always contrives to thrust its nose into every man's house when there is anything to be got."

The Rev. J. G. Wood thinks there were extenuating circumstances for the rudeness.

The Watertons fared but badly in the stormy times of the Reformation, and, preferring conscience to property, they retained their ancient faith, but lost heavily in this world's goods. The many coercive acts against Roman Catholics naturally had their effect, not only on those who actually lived in the time of the Reformation, but upon their successors. A Roman Catholic could not sit in Parliament, he could not hold a commission in the army, he could not be a justice of the peace, he had to pay double land tax, and to think himself fortunate if he had any land left on which taxes could be demanded. He was not allowed to keep a horse worth more than five pounds, and more irritating than all, he had either to attend the parish church or to pay twenty pounds for every month of absence. In fact, a Roman Catholic was looked upon and treated as a wholly inferior being and held much the same relative position to his persecutors as Jews held toward the Normans and Saxons in the times of the Crusades. . . . Waterton was, during some of his best years, a personal sufferer from these acts, and they rankled too deeply in his mind to be forgotten. Hence the repeated and most irrelevant allusions in his writings to Martin Luther, Henry VIII,

Queen Bess, Archbishop Cranmer, Oliver Cromwell, Charles Stuart, "Dutch William" (mostly associated with the "Hanoverian rat" and the national debt), and other personages celebrated in history. . . . On principle he refused to qualify as Deputy-Lieutenant and magistrate, because he had been debarred from doing so previously to the Emancipation Act.

Charles Waterton was born on the ancestral domain of Walton in 1782. He was the twenty-seventh Lord of Walton; and, through his father's mother, ninth in descent from Blessed Thomas More, the martyred Chancellor of Henry VIII. The estate, no longer in the possession of the Watertons, is some three miles outside of the village of Wakefield and not far from Leeds. When he was ten, he was sent to Tudhoe, a village near Durham, to a private school conducted by a Catholic priest. This little school had a remote and very slight connection with Ushaw College, on the strength of which Waterton is sometimes erroneously described as having belonged to that college. The article on Ushaw in the *Catholic Encyclopedia* does not include him among its distinguished sons. At the age of fourteen, he entered Stonyhurst where he remained for four years and completed his formal education. The Watertons had given several members to the Society of Jesus: they lie under ancient tombstones in the shadow of the chapel of Stonyhurst. The traditional affection of the Watertons toward the Jesuits was deepened in Charles as a result of his four years with them. Through a long life he eagerly sought every opportunity of testifying in public and private to his affectionate reverence for them. One of his instructors, Father Clifford, a first cousin of Lord Clifford, noting the young naturalist's tendency to range abroad—sometimes beyond bounds— questing for field knowledge in his little private pursuit, thought he saw in him a budding Englishman whose adventurous spirit would probably lead him out of his snug island home into trackless places at the ends of the earth. As a safeguard in such a contingency, he asked young Waterton to promise that he would never touch wine or intoxicating liquor. This promise Charles made and kept to the end of his life.

After leaving Stonyhurst, with accomplishments that included facility in writing Latin verse and a love of English and Latin literature, he spent two years at home with his father, during which time he acquired the reputation of being the most daring rider with the Lord Darlington foxhounds. In 1802, he went to Spain and had a wild year of cholera and earthquakes, ending in a mad dash for home on a sailing vessel. A bold skipper had been found, who was willing to defy a cordon of brigs-of-war, maintaining a strict embargo on the shipping of Malaga. The weakened condition of Waterton's health called for a gentler climate than that of Yorkshire, and in 1804 he voyaged to Demerara, British Guiana, on the sloping forehead of South America. It is close to the equator, and came into American notice prominently some years ago in the famous Venezuelan boundary dispute. Here the young naturalist took charge of two estates belonging to his father and uncle.

The death of his father two years later required his presence in England, but the new squire returned almost immediately to the tropics, where he continued in the administration of the estates for six years till the death of his uncle, when he was relieved of his double charge and felt free to indulge at leisure his pet hobby.

Then began the series of four journeys which are described in his famous book. Its full title indicates broadly the extent of the journeys and the years in which they were made: *Wanderings in South America, the North-West of the United States, and the Antilles in the Years 1812, 1816, 1820, and 1824.* The writer in the London *Times* to whom reference has been made, says that Waterton's style is baroque and the least modern part of him, calling attention especially, as Sydney Smith had done already, to the elaborate apostrophes and the classical allusions and quotations. Yet, he is forced to admit that they are oddly in keeping with the general structure, like the statues on the façade or roof of a building. With these outworn little tricks of rhetoric, the style is curiously moldproof and modern. "Many years ago," Mr. Charles Livingston Bull tells us, "when reading this book for the first time, my boyish imagination was so fired that I determined the first opportunity should find me on my way to Waterton's beloved Demerara, and in March of the year 1908, I sailed from New York on a journey in which I covered most of the country which he describes so well and so thor-

oughly." A dead or superannuated style is not so won-
der-working.

While Waterton in his kindly and simple-hearted
fashion, and probably under the influence of Sterne,
makes expansive and flourishing gestures, he could be
terse enough on occasion, and he possessed no mean
mastery of the "difficult art of omission," by means of
which, if we believe Stevenson, it is possible to make an
Iliad out of the ordinary issue of a daily newspaper.
The *Times* critic admits that in one respect Waterton
was thoroughly modern in having a journalist's eye for
good "copy," and he cites the well-known adventure
with a cayman. A cayman, or caiman, is a word one
seldom hears now, and is the name of the larger species
of alligator.

It would be an easy task to write the headlines with which report-
ers would diversify the stories they got from him. Indeed, many of
them would have been cabled from Para or Georgetown to New
York or London, and would have flared through the press of the
world. One of his stories survives in its pristine sensationalism.
Overnight a caiman had taken a hooked bait attached to a rope, and
Waterton wished to catch it alive. His people had the end of the
rope and were ordered to pull the reptile toward the shore. Waterton's first idea was to thrust a mast into its mouth, thus making it
harmless; but as the creature drew near, lashing the water in rage,
he made a sudden plunge, leaped on its back, pulled up its forelegs
to "serve as a bridle," and in this heroic posture the pair were
dragged out of the water and some forty yards over the sand. There
is no reasonable doubt that the story was true, although it lost nothing in the telling.

The writer goes on to give other instances of Waterton's instinctive feeling for whatever would be of lively interest to readers. Among them he quotes the classic description of the sloth, the first accurate description of that strange beast in literature. This was the description which moved Sydney Smith to make a memorable comparison: "The sloth moves suspended, rests suspended, sleeps suspended, and passes his whole life in suspense, like a young clergyman distantly related to a bishop."

It is in this volume that Waterton enters an eloquent defense of the Jesuits against the stereotyped Protestant representations of Southey in his *History of Brazil*. He also showed himself rather careless of a certain phase of English temper by speaking kindly and sympathetically of Irish endurance under English misrule; and almost equally careless of the same temper by liking and praising Americans. Of all the famous English visitors to the United States, he is perhaps the only writer among them who met us and liked us and did not regard us from a lofty and superior eminence when telling his countrymen about us. Wilson's *Ornithology of the United States* was the book which induced Waterton to go by way of New York on his fourth and last trip to Demerara. He saw the Hudson up to Albany, went across the state to Buffalo, visited Montreal and Quebec, and on his return to New York stopped at Lake George and Saratoga, "a gay and fashionable place," where he enjoyed the hotels, the waters, and the company.

There is a pleasing frankness, and ease and becoming dignity, in the American ladies; and the good humor, and absence of all haughtiness and puppyism in the gentlemen, must, no doubt, impress the traveler with elevated notions of the company who visit this celebrated spa.

Of course he went to Philadelphia, where Wilson's *Ornithology* had been printed. His comment on the city is interesting.

Travelers hesitate whether to give the preference to Philadelphia or to New York. Philadelphia is certainly a noble city, and its environs beautiful; but there is a degree of quiet and sedateness in it, which, though no doubt very agreeable to the man of calm and domestic habits, is not so attractive to one of speedy movements.

Waterton studied men more than birds while he was here. We must have been a rather crude nation in 1824, and yet Waterton has nothing but hearty approval of us, excepting for our habit of smoking. We still have the habit, but it is no longer especially characteristic. Waterton's portrait of us may be flattering beyond our deserts; still it bears a more convincing air of being related to some sort of reality than do the caricatures and provincial burlesque of Moore and Dickens and the loose impressionisms of their successors. It took at least courage, not to mention other virtues, to write and publish the following observation about the American:

He has certainly hit upon the way (but I could not make out by what means) of speaking a much purer English language than that which is in general spoken on the parent soil. This astonished me much; but it is really the case.

He bids us farewell in a kindly and generous spirit:

Politicians of other countries imagine that intestine feuds will cause a division in this commonwealth; at present there appears to be no reason for such a conjecture. Heaven forbid that it should happen! The world at large would suffer by it. For ages yet to come, may this great commonwealth continue to be the United States of North America.

It is good to know that, if there are Englishmen like Mr. Kipling and the editor of the *National Review*, there are also Englishmen like Charles Waterton.

After the publication of the *Wanderings*, Waterton settled down and married. His wife died a year after marriage. Her two maiden sisters thereupon yielded to the bereaved husband's wishes and took over the care of his household, which now included an infant son. This arrangement continued in force till Waterton's death forty years later. We see henceforth the country squire instead of the intrepid explorer; though the naturalist still remains uppermost. He is said to have been the first to create a bird sanctuary by building a stone wall three miles in circumference and some eight or nine feet high around his park, besides making other elaborate provisions for protecting animal life and studying its habits. The results of his studies were published in a series of three volumes, interspersed with quaint bits of informal biography. His house stood on an island, approached by a single bridge, where the water birds could be watched from a window. The park was a paradise for all living things except the unfortunate Hanoverian rat. There were frequent excursions to the Continent in the company of the two sisters, and Stonyhurst was regularly a port of call, especially during the Christmas season.

It would be hard to imagine a happier life. But it was not the life of an epicure. The hardy habits of the wilderness persisted. Norman Moore, who lived with him toward the end, gives the squire's morning order: it is substantially the same as that given by Dr. Hobson:

He went to bed early, and slept upon the bare floor, with a block of wood for his pillow. He rose for the day at half-past three, and spent the hour from four to five at prayer in his chapel. He then read every morning a chapter in a Spanish life of St. Francis Xavier, followed by a chapter of *Don Quixote* in the original, after which he used to stuff birds or write letters till breakfast.

Breakfast was at eight. The Spartan quality of this régime cannot be fully appreciated unless one has experienced the chill of an English winter morning in an unheated house, and has been informed that Waterton's early life in the tropics had made him delicately sensitive to cold. He hardly ever ate meat; his wildest indulgence was a cup of tea; he used to vex the good Doctor Hobson by rigorously observing all the fast days of the Church long after he had passed the age limit set for fasting. He had another habit which appalled the doctor. When Waterton was a young man and about to penetrate alone wild forests far from the medical resources of civilization, he induced a surgeon to teach him how to open and close a vein so that he could bleed himself in an emergency; bleeding, by venesection, or by the application of leeches, was still the universal remedy for nearly every sort of ailment in the early days of the past century. Blood-letting became Waterton's panacea. Even in his eighties he would not hesitate to "take away from twenty to twenty-four ounces of blood, with not merely temporary freedom from all suffering, but with all the permanent benefit that could be desired." So writes Doctor Hobson in amazement. He could open and close a vein with either hand. Sometimes the knife was too much dulled by casual use about the house, and had to be sharpened after a futile attempt (in Waterton's phrase) "to tap the claret." Let modern science shake its incredulous head!

The athlete's joy in overcoming difficulties, which started him on early adventure, was something he never lost. When he was over forty, he climbed to the top of the cross on St. Peter's in Rome, and left his glove on the point of the lightning rod. Pope Pius VII thought the glove impaired the usefulness of the lightning rod and ordered its removal. As no one was eager to assume the task, Waterton had to repeat his feat "to the amusement of his friends and the delight of the populace." He also climbed to the top of the castle of St. Angelo and stood with one foot on the head of the angel. When he was over eighty, he could clamber to the top of the highest oaks in his park. After this, the feats of the young men, who are the "human flies" of the "movies," must appear tame. These well-authenticated accounts lend color to a Stonyhurst legend of Waterton's school days. Once, in that juvenile mood which is the terror of fond parents, he proceeded to prove to some of his schoolboy friends that he could climb the face of the tower at the entrance of the college. The tower, built in the days of James I, rises in four courses of pillars one above another. Waterton had reached the fourth and highest course, and was preparing to negotiate a selected pillar when Father Rector appeared on the scene far below, and, to the disgust of everybody, peremptorily ordered the lad to descend at once. That night a storm blew down the very pillar Waterton was preparing to leg up when the Rector interfered. An examination of the fallen pillar disclosed the fact that there was an old crack straight through it, and it had been in such perilous condition that a slight jar would have overthrown it. The mended pillar has been restored to its place and serves to point a moral for succeeding generations.

Modern science would probably like to know the secret of Waterton's pliability of limb in old age. The years forgot to harden his arteries. "When Mr. Waterton was seventy-seven years of age," says Dr. Hobson, "I was witness to his scratching the back part of his head with the big toe of his right foot." And, again the doctor's own words must be given, "in the summer of 1861, when in his seventy-ninth year, Mr. Waterton, in one of his jocose moods, by a run of fifteen yards, bounded over a stout wire fence, without touching it hand or foot, and this I carefully measured to three feet six inches in height." A Stonyhurst tradition—not a loud, boastful tradition: rather a shocked and somewhat politely modulated tradition—tells how the old naturalist would be as likely as not to enter a room full of company during the holidays, walking on his hands. What a terrible old man! Still, with all his informal ways, no one, we are told, felt like taking liberties with the squire.

Stonyhurst is a rich field for the lover of Waterton. In its museum he can see the identical cayman which Waterton rode, together with the wooden hook and rope used on the famous occasion. Here, too, is a finely preserved sloth; and indeed, a large collection of specimens preserved by the naturalist's own hands and according to a formula of his own, which he claimed to be superior to every known process of taxidermic art practiced in his day. Latin inscriptions in pentameter verse, of Waterton's composition, often take the place of the usual learned labels. One semicircular case is said by Dr. Hobson to have been the main ornament of the Waterton home. The general inscription of the exhibit in this case is: "England's Reformation Zoölogically Illustrated." A beautifully crested bird rests on a perch above a small fragment of granite inscribed,

"The Catholic Church Triumphant: *Tu es Petrus,* etc."
In front and below is a repulsive-looking crab, marked
"Mother Law Church," with eight villainous beetles,
denominated "her dissenting fry." On the right is a big,
bloated, and hideous horned-toad, with a crested tail,
which we are informed is Henry VIII. To the left,
another fat toad, not charming by any means, stands
for "Dutch William III." Bishop Burnet, "The Rev."
John Knox, Old Nick, Archbishop Cranmer, Titus
Oates, and Queen Bess are represented by loathsome
subterraneous specimens of crawling animal life. There
is a rumor that a temporary coolness sprang up between
Waterton and Stonyhurst when the Rector of the college hesitated to manifest enthusiastic appreciation at
the offer of this particular exhibit.

Norman Moore's account of Waterton's last days de-
serves reproduction.

After breakfast we went with a carpenter to finish some bridges at
the far end of the park. The work was completed, and we were pro-
ceeding homewards when, in crossing a small bridge, a bramble
caught the squire's foot, and he fell heavily upon a log. He was
greatly shaken, and said he thought he was dying. He walked, not-
withstanding, a little way, and was then compelled to lie down. He
would not permit his sufferings to distract his mind, and he pointed
out to the carpenter some trees that were to be felled. He presently
continued his route, and managed to reach the spot where the boat
was moored. Hitherto he had refused all assistance, but he could
not step from the bank into the boat and he said, "I am afraid I
must ask you to help me in." He walked from the landing place
into the house, changed his clothes, and came and sat in the large
room below. The pain increasing, he rose from his seat after he

had seen his doctor, and though he had been bent double with anguish, he persisted in walking upstairs without help, and would have gone to his room in the top story, if, for the sake of saving trouble to others, he had not been induced to stop halfway in the sitting room of his sister-in-law. . . . The pain abated, and the next day he seemed better. In the afternoon he talked to me a good deal, chiefly about natural history. But he was well aware of his perilous condition, for he remarked to me, "This is a bad business," and later on he felt his pulse often, and said, "It is a bad case." He was more than self-possessed. A benignant cheerfulness beamed from his mind, and in spite of fits of pain he frequently looked up with a gentle smile, and made some little joke. Toward midnight he grew worse. The priest was summoned, and Waterton got ready to die. He pulled himself upright without help, sat in the middle of the sofa, and gave his blessing in turn to his grandson, Charles, to his granddaughter, Mary, to each of his sisters-in-law, to his niece, and to myself, and left a message for his son who was hastening back from Rome. He then received the last Sacraments, repeated all the responses, Saint Bernard's hymn in English, and the first two verses of *Dies Irae*. The end was now at hand, and he died at twenty-seven minutes past two in the morning of May 27, 1865.

The death of the squire was a calamity to his tenants and all the countryside, to Protestants and Catholics alike; for he was bountiful in his charity irrespective of creed. He disliked Protestantism thoroughly, but he could love those who practiced it in good faith. Englishmen who differed with him in religion, and suffered from his irony, were willing to accept Thackeray's judgment as final, that "he was a good man; his works were made to square with his faith, he dined on a crust, lived as chastely as a hermit, and gave his all to the poor."

The Thackeray episode in Rome, a touching evidence of Waterton's strong faith and his affection for his friends, ought to be coupled with another illustrating his love of dumb animals. It was his custom before going out on his afternoon walk to provide himself with a crust against chance meetings with some of his animal friends. One goose, especially, used to wait for him hopefully every evening at the end of the bridge over the moat. Norman Moore was with Waterton one day when the usual crust had been forgotten. On approaching the bridge, the squire hung back. He looked troubled. "How shall we ever get past that goose?" and there was worry in his voice. The lord of the manor thereupon adopted the Fabian strategy of skulking among distant trees on various pretexts, with much reconnoitering of the bridge, till Mariana at the moat got tired waiting and waddled off. He could not bear, says Moore, "to give it nothing when it raised its bill."

Eminence in art and science does not often surpass itself in the most difficult art of all, that of life. And that is Charles Waterton's chief distinction. The sturdy Yorkshire squire was of a different type from that of the Oxford-bred Newman. But both men meet on a high plane of personal holiness, and in the grace of a Faith superior to all the challenges of the world, the flesh, and the devil. Excepting always the easy masters of fame, the student of literature is often at a loss to explain the survival of the chosen few in the deluge of oblivion which blots out the writers of every generation. If a guess be allowed on the survival of Waterton, it would be concerned more with his personality than with his literary qualities: though it cannot be a common-place style which lets an interesting man shine through. In these pelagian days, so busy upon the old futility of making conduct keep an upright position without super-natural supports, the wholesome personality of Charles Waterton can raise the average of sanity and cheerful-ness on the favorite bookshelf.

SIR THOMAS MORE: SAINT AND HUMORIST

"THE great," says Emerson in his pontifical way, "will not condescend to take anything seriously: all must be as gay as the song of a canary though it were the building of cities or the eradication of old and foolish churches and nations which have cumbered the earth long thousands of years." Still, when he wishes to illustrate this doctrine by example, the only one in all Christendom to occur to him is Thomas More, who literally laid down his life to prevent an old Church from being eradicated and supplanted by a new one. Which of those two Churches is foolish, the old one or the new, is a question which, if it has not already been settled, may be confidently left for sure solution to the processes of time. The entire paragraph, the brightest in the essay on "Heroism," leaves a strong impression of having been written with Sir Thomas More in mind. "That which takes my fancy most in the heroic class is the good humor and hilarity they exhibit. It is a height to which the common duty can very well attain, to suffer and to dare with solemnity. But these rare souls set opinion, success, and life at so cheap a rate that they will not soothe their enemies by petitions, or the show of sorrow, but wear their habitual greatness." His intuition, so often more reliable than his erratic play of intellect, brings the "sage of Concord" very close to a great spiritual truth when he goes on to say that, if we could see the whole race assembled together, the true heroes would appear "like little children frolicking together, though to the eyes of mankind at large they wear a stately and solemn garb of works and influence."

The only portion of mankind which, as a class, answers to this description are the saints. It was from the saints accordingly that Emerson, with some reluctance we may suppose, selected his type of debonair and smiling hero. Blessed Thomas More was a leading statesman and politician; the first great writer of English prose; a classicist of European reputation; a philosopher, a theologian, an original thinker, a man of affairs, an eloquent pleader, a skilful parliamentarian, an honest and learned judge, a smooth and astute ambassador, and the principal adviser of a powerful monarch. It sounds preposterously fortunate. But there it stands in history with more than the usual explicitness and corroboration.

Indeed, on the evidence this is, if anything, an incomplete catalogue of the greatness of the immediate successor to that Wolsey, "who once trod the ways of glory." Nevertheless, we should look for Sir Thomas More in the "nurseries of heaven." His judicial ermine and gold chains and seals of office, the royal patronage and the homage of the Commons, the respectful and almost affectionate deference of scholars and nobles, could not induce him to take the world seriously. He proceeded on his shining way with the quizzical and detached and amused air of a curious stranger on Broadway or in the Strand, or rather like a sprightly child sent out into the country for a maying, with a keen relish for the beautiful things of life, conditioned, of course, in the expectation of a lasting City at nightfall. He glances athwart his generation like a happy and exotic being from some superior planet. His shy and subtle aloofness from the world, whose history he was making, marked him out for official beatification more surely than his martyrdom. His mask of gentle laughter still baffles the curious scrutiny of eyes that are worldly.

It is fascinating to observe how his jests multiplied with his misfortunes, as if these were your true material for comedy. When his greatness fell about him he sat among the ruins, shaking with a quiet merriment, as if the greatest joke in life had at last been perpetrated. The clouds gathering so darkly over him served no other purpose than to display the sheet-lightning of his humor. Wolsey in a similar, though less serious, situation became for all time a tragic figure. Neither history nor legend has been able to employ the properties of tragedy in the last act of Sir Thomas More's life. He whistled tragedy down all the winds with a fine and genuine unconcern. He refused to live up to the traditions of prosperity in swift collapse, of virtue in bondage and misery, of merit trampled under foot. The spectacle which he exhibits excites no pity nor terror. In Aristotle's phrase, it purifies the heart, indeed: but with feelings of serenest joy.

Only once do tears leap to our eyes: it is when his beloved daughter, Meg, meets him on the Thames landing at the tower, just after sentence of death has been passed upon him, and breaks her way through the spectators and the soldiers to fling herself upon him with passionate tears, and, after pitiful hands have loosed her grasp of him, tears herself away from those who would hold her and rushes back to embrace him again and again for the last time. The night before his execution her father wrote Meg a letter. They had, long months before, deprived him of writing material, and he had been using coal for pen and ink, finding his paper where he might. He had assured Meg that pecks of coal could not suffice to express his love for her, and now in this last letter he tells her that he never loved her so much as on that day, a week ago, when she clung to him and kissed him on the Tower-wharf.

This lovely human touch was necessary to complete the true impression of his humor and to save it from the suspicion of a proud disdain, thoughtless, as well as heartless, of the claims of life. For, it must be admitted, his high spirits which seemed to rise with the increasing imminence of death, almost disconcert a strict sense of the proprieties. A woman in the crowd that surged about him on his progress to the place of execution, cried to him about some papers she had intrusted to his keeping when he was Lord High Chancellor. "My good woman, allow me half an hour and his gracious majesty, our good King, will relieve me of all responsibility for your papers." He bade the friendly lieutenant of the Tower to be of good cheer, for they would all "be merry" together in heaven. When the scaffold was reached he showed droll alarm at its poor construction and tested the insecure steps leading up to it. He begged the lieutenant very gravely to help him up those crazy stairs. "As for my coming down," he said, "let me shift for myself." How could the woebegone lieutenant remain serious? The apparatus and customary trappings of the tragedy were made ridiculous.

On mounting the scaffold Sir Thomas asked the assembled people to pray for him, and told them simply and briefly that he died in and for the holy Catholic Church. He then called the attention of the axman to the shortness of his neck, urging him to be careful of his professional credit. After he had laid his head upon the block he stopped proceedings for a moment or two that he might dispose his beard safely from the axe, since, he said, it was not accused of treason.

The Protestant bishop, Burnet, an historian of the Reformation, was shocked at what he was pleased to consider the levity of Sir Thomas on this momentous occasion. It is true, most of us do well "to suffer and to dare with solemnity." When death confronts us we cannot hope, and perhaps ought not to desire, to be in a mood for jesting, unless we have a record like Sir Thomas's behind us. Compunction and fear are the proper and familiar sentiments of a Christian living and dying; and the most jaundiced critic of Sir Thomas More dare not hint that he ever yielded to the easy refreshment of pagan anodynes such as shallow levity, smug self-complacence, arbitrary optimism, or the illusions of a presumptuous hope. The hero and the ascetic are not always the gentle practitioners of a playful and charming humor. Human nature has to be nagged into decency: it has to be whipped with scorpions into the front line of saints and heroes; and it sometimes becomes grim under the discipline. The bright and warm comforts are so much the ordinary conditions of genial humor that when a saint smiles without self-consciousness, the remarkable phenomenon seems to demand some sort of explanation.

Has anyone noted that Coleridge's theory of humor appears to promise some light which will help us to understand how seriousness and merriment, if carried to their logical limits, meet at a common point? "There is always," he says, "in a genuine humor an acknowledgment of the hollowness and farce of the world, and its disproportion to the godlike within us." And he proceeds to make the essence of humor to consist "in a certain reference to the general and the universal, by which the finite great is brought into identity with the little, or the little with the finite great, so as to make both nothing in comparison with the infinite. The little is made great, and the great little, in order to destroy both; because all is equal in contrast with the infinite." Precisely: to Sir Thomas his beard was of as much importance as his head, or, if you wish to put it differently, his head was of as small importance as his beard, because he was thinking of the Infinite.

If Coleridge's analysis of humor has anything in it, one can perhaps see how it may be possible to be a humorist without being a saint; but it is not easy to see how anyone can be a saint without being a humorist. It would seem that solid and sober persons who are dismayed at the quips and quirks of the saints, are not what you might call good psychologists of either sanctity or humor.

It comes to this: if serious people are tempted to fling up their hands at the casual air with which saints trifle with misfortune, it is only because serious people are not serious enough. Take, for instance, Bishop Burnet. It is very probable that he did not wear a hair-shirt most of his life, nor get up every morning at two o'clock to spend most of the time in prayer and the rest in study till seven o'clock Mass. Thomas More did these things and many other hard things like them, which it is scarcely an injustice to the bishop to surmise that he never dreamed of doing. It is not, therefore, idle or paradoxical to conclude that Sir Thomas was the more serious man. If anyone is frivolous, it must be the worthy bishop who shakes his head sadly over Sir Thomas's willful sport with the mournful properties of a melancholy occasion. It has to be admitted in the bishop's favor that nearly all of Sir Thomas's world shook their sadly puzzled heads over him. You could never tell, say contemporaries, whether he was fooling or in earnest. Imagine their bewilderment when they beheld him cracking jokes in an imprisonment which he need not endure and on a scaffold which he need not have mounted, if he would only take a trifle of an oath which practically all England had swallowed without winking. Outward appearances proclaimed him a *farceur* to most of the practical and sensible people of the day.

Even his wife, the estimable Alice Middleton, was on Bishop Burnet's side in her opinion of her husband's want of seriousness. Watch her in a famous passage from William Roper's delightful life of his father-in-law: "When Sir Thomas More had continued a good while in the Tower, my lady, his wife, obtained license to see him, who at her first coming, like a simple woman and somewhat worldly, too, with this manner of salutations, bluntly saluted him, 'What the good year, Mr. More,' quoth she, 'I marvel that you, that have been always hitherto taken for so wise a man, will now play the fool to lie here in a filthy prison and be content to be shut up among mice and rats when you might be abroad at your liberty, and with the favor and good will of the King and his Council, if you would do as all the bishops and best learned of his Realm have done. And seeing you have at Chelsea a right fair house,

your library, your books, your gallery, your garden,
your orchards, and all other necessaries so handsomely
about you, where you might, in the company of me,
your wife, your children, and household be merry, I
muse what in God's name, you mean here still thus
fondly to tarry.' After he had a while quietly heard
her, with a cheerful countenance he said unto her, 'I
pray thee, good Mrs. Alice, tell me one thing.' 'What
is that?' quoth she. 'Is not this house as nigh heaven as
mine own?' To whom she, after her accustomed fashion, not liking such talk, answered, 'Tilly vally, tilly
vally.' 'How say you, Mrs. Alice, is it not so?' quoth
he. 'Bone Deus, bone Deus, man, will this gear never
be left?' quoth she."

Poor lady! As Francis Thompson observes, it is a
grievous trial to be the near relation of a saint. To
Alice, who thought of the infinite only when she said
her prayers, the too obvious difference between the
pleasant park in Chelsea and the moldy cell in the
Tower was not a proper subject for curious and patient
speculation. I dare say Sir Thomas could not help being
amused at her stout opposition, but I am sure also that
her distress stretched him on a rack crueler than any in
the Tower. It was not in the nature of his humor to
inflict pain or draw satisfaction from any exhibition of
it. When the lieutenant of the Tower announced with
much confusion and embarrassment that sorely against
his will he was obliged, by the King's strict command,
to cut down the comforts and small liberties of his illus-

trious prisoner, Sir Thomas put him in countenance with a laugh and a jest: "Assure yourself, Mr. Lieutenant, I do not mislike my cheer; but whenever I do so, then thrust me out of your doors."

The Commissioners, his former friends and associates, who thought it best for worldly considerations to bend before the royal will and condemn him to death, were not elated over the performance of their task. Their pusillanimity might have stirred the scorn and contempt of a less sweet-tempered man than the doomed prisoner. The concluding portion of his speech to them shows us which of them, in Sir Thomas's mind, he or his judges, was in need of consoling words. "More have I not to say, my Lords, but like as the Blessed Apostle, St. Paul, as we read in the Acts of the Apostles, was present and consented to the death of St. Stephen, and kept their clothes that stoned him to death, and yet be they now both twain holy saints in heaven, and shall continue there friends forever, so I verily trust and shall right heartily pray, that though your Lordships have now on earth been judges to my condemnation, we may yet hereafter in heaven merrily all meet together to our everlasting salvation."

The thought of the Infinite, it will be noticed, was always with him, not only conferring the gift of humor but also preserving it from the common form of degeneration into cynicism and sardonic irony. While the sun was shining on his side of the globe, he took no credit for seeing the way while antipodeans walked in darkness. He thanked the God of light and was humbled by the privilege.

Nor did he feel tempted to flaunt his privilege as a challenge. The consciences of others were not in his keeping and the issue for which he was laying down his life was, at that time, somewhat subtle for the common mind. He needed all his energy and attention for the struggle going on in his own soul that truth and justice might triumph over selfish casuistry and the fear of consequence. He sought to win no followers, even in his own family. He uttered no defiance, but walked warily, as might be expected of the shrewdest lawyer of that time, among the cunning snares of an angry King and a scorned Queen. Perjury had at last to be suborned to undo him.

Sir Thomas was of a gentle and sensitive cast of character, with a scholar's and a cultivated man's extreme dislike of violence. He shrank in all his instincts from this rough contest with the Royal Supremacy, and was troubled by the doubt whether he would be granted the grace and the strength to stand by his conscience to the end. When the end actually arrived, he was surprised at the absence of all fear. The relief and exhilaration of that surprise made him more than usually mirthful, and accordingly enigmatic to people who hold that martyrs must be fanatics. Bishop Burnet called him a buffoon, since he could not call him a fanatic. The Blessed Thomas must enjoy this.

After all, where is the conundrum? As he had lived,

so Sir Thomas died—a common fate enough—measuring the finite with the Infinite. Contrary to his humble expectations, he brought to the experience of dying the same buoyant spirit which he had brought to the business of living, with some extra zest thrown in because he was so near Home after a delightful day.

SIR THOMAS MORE: THE SPIRITUAL WRITER

In the summer of 1534 Sir Thomas More lay confined in the Tower of London waiting until such time as Henry might deem it opportune to put him to death. They had not yet deprived him of books and writing paper, and he spent the hours of his captivity very pleasantly, when he was not praying, in composing a spiritual treatise. He beheld the stately and massive edifice of the Catholic Church in England, reared by the sanctities, martyrdoms, and holy aspirations of a thousand years, shaken to the verge of collapse. No one in England, or elsewhere, not even the tyrant, Henry himself, saw so clearly the march of events toward national apostacy as this shrewd lawyer and appraiser of men.

His clairvoyance is somewhat of a mystery today. Externally, the Church seemed to be much the same as ever. The King's quarrel with the Pope would probably blow over as so many similar quarrels had done in the past. Besides, kings did not live forever, and quarrels of this kind were not commonly transmitted to heirs and successors. It seemed to the European statesmen of the time to be no more than a rather serious diplomatic tiff, which would readjust itself in the usual way. One could almost succeed in discovering a defence for this light-hearted view of the situation in the subsequent course of events, when the Church was so often apparently on the point of retrieving her fallen fortunes, but for some slight mischance due to incredible blundering or misunderstanding. While the late Chancellor was languishing in the Tower, the ministers and monasteries were still intact, Catholic churchmen were in honor, the Church was functioning through countless parishes, the Catholic life of England bore all the signs of vigor. It was inconceivable, one might suppose, that the knell of doom was sounding for this glorious Church.

But so it was. Sir Thomas knew it, and he was the only man who knew. Was it because he, better than anyone else, understood the formidable nature of the conspiracy of wealth and political influence organized by greed against the Church? Did he alone detect the symptoms of deadly decay in a hierarchical structure long exposed to the corrosive action of secular interference and favoritism? Was he the only one keen enough to appreciate the fearful force of the impact of imported heresies and revolts upon a powerful middle class which had been scandalized and rendered cynically critical by the worldliness of courtier-prelates? Whatever the signs in the heaven during the halcyon and deceptive calm, he, of all the statesmen in Europe, read them as harbingers of a devastating hurricane. Whether he realized that the destruction would be so thorough and so irreparable as the event proved, there is, perhaps, no means of determining. But his deductions and forebodings, the oppressive sense of great and impending calamity, as they urge themselves to the surface in the spiritual book written during the first months of his imprisonment, cannot but strike the modern reader with something of the force of inspired prophecy.

The title given to the treatise by Sir Thomas is, *A Dialogue of Comfort Against Tribulation, Made by a Hungarian in Latin, and Translated out of Latin into French, and out of French into English.* The setting of the dialogue is the house of a certain Anthony in the city of Buda. Anthony is a virtuous and respected citizen who has grown old in the service of the State, and now, in his declining years, has nothing to do except to engage himself serenely in the more immediate preparation for a happy death. All the portents of the times point to an imminent invasion of the Turks and the violent persecution of all good Christian people who value their Faith more than the whole world. A prey to the prevalent apprehensions, Anthony's nephew, Vincent, pays several visits to his uncle to gather from the old gentleman's wisdom and ripe experience fortifying counsels against the approaching trials. This is the simple framework on which are spread the hopes and fears and most intimate self-communings of a great man at the most critical moment in his life.

The framework also serves as disguise. Here we have again the Sir Thomas of the *Utopia*, a liberty-loving man obliged in an age of absolutism to veil his ideas under fictitious forms. Plain speaking was not always an easy virtue in those days. When tyrants had to be crossed, it was sometimes a heroism; and, when his conscience urged it, it was a form of heroism which Sir Thomas was not afraid to practice. In the *tracasseries* of courts, where envy and jealousy were ever on the alert to entangle honesty in the coils and technicalities of the law, the man who desired to raise the windows and to induce a circulation of new and healthy ideas, had to pick his way nicely. The *Utopia* was a challenge and a criticism which would have brought Sir Thomas's head to the block ere his career was well started, had it been couched in plain terms. As it is, we are a little surprised today that it succeeded in passing off as well as it did. Sir Thomas clearly entertained an almost cynically low opinion of popular powers of penetration. Similarly, we are astonished that the transparent disguise of the *Dialogue of Comfort* could have succeeded in deceiving the dullest of official censors.

What imaginable reason was there for issuing a book in England on the religious troubles of remote Hungary? The Turkish peril in the Balkans, although serious in that day as it has been in our own, is, nevertheless, no particular occasion for a minute and anxious survey of the spiritual resources of Christianity on the part of an Englishman waiting for execution in the Tower of London. How could the censor have failed to pause over this sentence: "For there is no born Turk so cruel to Christian folk as is the false Christian that falleth from the Faith"? The only plausible explanation of the density of the officials, who missed so egregiously the real nature and point of the book, is that Henry had not yet exposed to the world the native ferocity of his temper. He had been up to this a rather good-natured monarch. It is probable that he himself was unaware of certain black possibilities in the recesses of his heart, and as yet had not the faintest notion of the fearful upheaval which was to follow in the train of his head-strong passions.

The ex-Chancellor must have had a profound insight into the character of his sovereign. English Catholics were never in so great need of fortifying counsels to prepare them for an overwhelming avalanche of ad-versity. And yet the tempest was so far below the hori-zon of the average man, with its annihilating menace so completely hidden from the common view, that the most brilliant and intellectual Englishman living at the time could send out a solemn warning and endeavor to prepare his countrymen against disaster without being suspected of his real design, simply because he em-ployed the rather crude device of putting his words in the mouth of an imaginary character and transferring the outlook from England to Hungary. Sir Thomas was neither by nature nor untoward fortune a prophet of evil. He may be described as the wittiest, most genial, and most successful man of his day. It was in a way characteristic of his clever genius, since he felt impelled to accept the rôle of Jeremias, to utter his lamentations in as light a note as possible. Sir Thomas could not help being merry. When a little subtlety was needed to throw treason-hunting censors off the track, he must have reveled in the expedient of merriment.

The historical significance of the *Dialogue of Comfort* will, perhaps, constitute its chief interest for the general reader. It leads us into the penetralia of a statesman's mind at a crisis when the world, of which he was a foremost figure, was undergoing an epochal transformation. But it would be an error to suppose that the value of the work is merely documentary. It is beyond any doubt one of the most charming spiritual treatises in the English language. It is divided into three books, of which the contents may be roughly outlined as follows: I. The Function of Suffering in Human Life; II. Various and Common Kinds of Affliction, Principally Temptations of the Soul, with Corresponding Remedies; III. Temporal Evils and the Way They Are to be Encountered. Under these broad headings is collected a mass of weighty practical philosophy garnered from a career unusually crowded with rich and multifarious experience, and presented with an instinct for literary form which, in England at least, was the most highly cultivated of the age. Like Sir Thomas himself, it is a synthesis of unexpected excellences, with surprises around every corner.

It is to be noted, too, that, while the *Dialogue* is intensely Catholic in tone, it carefully avoids all controversy. In this respect it is a singular exception among the writings of Sir Thomas in the vernacular. In a great nation abundantly supplied with an educated clergy, secular and regular, it is difficult to understand why his was about the only pen at the service of the Church to do battle in the vernacular against heresy. His antagonists were arrogantly confident at having the field of literature practically to themselves. They were men who felt no inconvenience in stooping to employ any coarse or ignoble means of discrediting the Church in the popular eye. Very often Sir Thomas was constrained to fight his adversaries with their own weapons. With a public just learning to read, personal invective went further than argument, and boisterous banter than nice appeals to feeling. This concession to the needs of the moment has seriously diminished the literary permanence of the martyr's polemical works in a language which has thrown all its favor on the side of his opponents, and has always regarded his as a lost cause. It remains a matter for regret that the merits of Sir Thomas More and of his rivals have not been weighed by literary critics in the same scales.

In the *Dialogue of Comfort*, however, Sir Thomas moves in a serene mountain atmosphere high above the brawlings and bickerings of the cities and congregations of men. He disengages himself from all petty strife and clamorous demands; and in the silence of an upland height beyond the clouds, holds deep converse with the sun and stars, with God and eternity. Strident echoes sometimes faintly reach him from the busy ant hills of men; but he refuses to be drawn from the spiritual regions of his thought.

"Holy St. Bernard giveth counsel that every man should make suit unto angels and saints to pray for him to God in the things that he would have sped at His holy hand. If any man will stick at that, and say it need not, because God can hear us Himself, and will also say that it is perilous so to do, because they say we be not so counseled by no Scripture, I will not dispute the matter here. He that will not do it, I hinder him not to leave it undone. But yet, for mine own part, I will as well trust to the counsel of St. Bernard, and reckon him for as good and as well learned in Scripture as any man that I hear say the contrary. And better dare I jeopard my soul with the soul of St. Bernard than with his that findeth that fault in his doctrine."

Although this is the farewell performance of Sir Thomas in the field of literature, written in a dungeon and in the very shadow of the scaffold and packed with reflections tinged by the light of a dawning eternity, his whimsical humor will assert itself. The easy and discursive style suggests a background of aged leisure in a country villa in the calm enjoyment of nature and pleasant surroundings. The author possesses his soul in peace while the axman is waiting, and through pages of most solemn import his natural laughter runs like a glistening thread.

Thus, in discussing the vivid and detailed realism of

dreams, Anthony, in a quizzical mood, defies young Vincent to prove that he is awake, and not merely dreaming. Vincent fumbles hopelessly and, finally, cries out in dismay: "God's Lord, uncle, you go now merrily to work with me, indeed, when you look and speak so sadly, and would make me ween I were asleep." When Vincent apologizes to his uncle for asking him to exhaust himself by so much talking, he elicits the following gem: "Nay, nay, good cousin, to talk much (except some other pain let me) is to be little grief. A fond old man is often as full of words as a woman. It is, you know well, as some poets paint us, all the lust of an old fool's life to sit well and warm with a cup and a roasted crab, and drivel and drink and talk." He then proceeds to tell a story about a nun who was being visited by her brother. The young man had just received his doctor's degree and had hastened to see his sister after his long absence at the university. When she was called to the grate and had presented her finger tips, she forthwith began to pronounce a long lecture on the vanity of the world in her gentle solicitude for her brother's soul.

"And gave him surely good counsel (saving somewhat too long) how he should be well aware in his living and master well his body for saving of his soul: and yet ere her own tale came all at an end, she began to find a little fault with him, and said: 'In good faith, brother, I do somewhat marvel that you that have been at learning so long, and are doctor, and so learned in the law of God, do not now at our meeting (while we meet so seldom) to me that am your sister and a simple unlearned soul give of your charity some fruitful exhortation. And as I doubt not but you can say some good thing yourself.' 'By my troth, good sister,' quoth her brother, 'I cannot for you, for your tongue hath never ceased, but said enough for us both.' "

Then there is the famous story of old Mother Maude, about the Ass and Wolf who came upon a time to confession to the Fox, and many another diverting tale. Sir Thomas liked to tell a good story. It is the Lord Chancellor, perhaps, who thinks it necessary to make apology: "As Pliny saith that there is no book lightly so bad but that some good thing a man may pick out thereof, so think I that there is almost no tale so foolish but that yet in one matter or other to some purpose it may hap to serve." We see why Erasmus loved this man, why he was the idol of his children, and why, ere his head was danced off by a royal mistress, he had to assume the mask of dullness to escape the exacting fondness of the King for his society.

And yet he seems to have been visited by pathetic little misgivings about the bubbling humor which there was not enough misfortune in the world to choke. Vincent is quoting Solomon and St. Thomas Aquinas in support of the contention that a man may sometimes search for comfort in tribulation at other sources, less spiritual than those hitherto enumerated by his uncle: "For a merry tale with a friend refresheth a man much, and without any harm lifteth his mind and amendeth his courage and his stomach, so that it seemeth but well done to take such recreation."

Anthony replies, and this time it is the saint and not the Lord Chancellor who speaks, that he thinks any counsel in favor of such comfort is superfluous, since it is a kind of comfort men are too prone to take of themselves. "You may see this by ourself, which coming now together to talk of as earnest, sad matter as men can devise, were fallen yet even at the first into wanton idle tales; and of truth, cousin, as you know well, myself am of nature even half a gigglot and more. I would I could as easily mend my fault as I well know it, but scant can I refrain it as old a fool as I am. Howbeit, so partial will I not be to my fault as to praise it. But for that you require my mind in the matter, whether men in tribulation may not lawfully seek recreation and comfort themselves with some honest mirth, first agreed that our chief comfort must be in God, and that with Him we must begin, and with Him continue, and with Him end also." He then settles the point in conformity with good and learned men who have allowed honest mirth as a concession to human weakness, too soon wearied, alas, by heavenly discourse. The argument is then clinched by another tale.

The rare literary quality of the style will not have escaped attention in the passages from the *Dialogue* already cited. A homely vigor of phrase, a swift penetration of mind, a balanced condition of judgment, and the

easy gesture of magnanimous humor give these pages a
Shakespearean flavor which epicurean palates will delight in. The large scroll of life lay unrolled before
the eyes of Sir Thomas, as before the eyes of the Eliza-
bethans, giving him some of that spacious outlook which
our literature was not to know again till some fifty years
after his death. Here, for instance, is a touch which
draws the modern and medieval worlds together.
Shakespeare could not have seen it, or he would have
stolen it. Anthony has been speaking of the cruel indulgence and false consolation which certain obsequious
pastors hold out to the wealthy members of their flocks.

"And in such wise deal they with him the rich man
as the mother doth sometimes with her child: Which
when the little boy will not rise in time for her, but lie
still abed and slug, and when he is up weepeth because
he hath lien so long, fearing to be beaten at school for
his late coming thither; she telleth him then that it is
but early days, and he shall come time enough, and
biddeth him, 'Go, good son, I warrant thee I have sent
to thy master myself; take thy bread and butter with
thee: thou shalt not be beaten at all.' And thus, so she
may send him merry forth at the door that he weep
not in her sight at home, she studieth not much upon
the matter though he be taken tardy and beaten when
he come to school."

What child has not been the victim of this gracious
perfidy? Again, speaking of the brief tenure of their
worldly estate, which prosperous folk enjoy, a favorite
topic with moralizing philosophers, the *Dialogue*

breaks into the following noble cadence:

"O cousin Vincent, if the whole world were animated with a reasonable soul (as Plato had weened it were) and that it had wit and understanding to mark and perceive all things, Lord God! how the ground on which a Prince buildeth his palace would loud laugh his lord to scorn, when he saw him proud of his possession, and heard him boast himself, that he and his blood are forever the very lords and owners of the land. For then would the ground think the while in himself: 'Ah, thou silly, poor soul, that weenest thou were half a god, and art amid thy glory but a man in a gay gown. I, that am the ground here over whom thou art so proud, have had a hundred such owners of me as thou callest thyself, more than ever thou hast heard the names of. And some of them that proudly went over mine head lie now low in my belly, and my side lieth over them. And many one shall, as thou doest now, call himself mine owner after thee, that neither shall be sib to thy blood, nor any word hear of thy name.' Who owned your castle, cousin, three thousand years ago?

"*Vincent:* 'Three thousand, uncle? Nay, nay, in any King, Christian or heathen, you may strike off a third part of that well enough, and as far as I ween half of the remnant, too. In far fewer years than three thousand it may well fortune that a poor ploughman's blood may come up to a kingdom; and a king's right royal kin on the other side fall down to the plough and cart; and neither that king know that ever he came from the cart, nor carter know that ever he came from the crown.' "

Does it seem extravagant to discover here for the first time in our literary history the genuine ancestry of that distinguished and dignified port and sad grave demeanor which glorify the prose of Milton, Sir Thomas Browne, Jeremy Taylor, DeQuincy, and Newman? And it is hard to believe that Thackeray, the genial satirist, could have read the famous description of the emptiness of fame without feeling kinship with Sir Thomas More.

"But now to speak of the thing itself in his own proper nature, what is it but a blast of another man's mouth, as soon passed as spoken? Whereupon he that setteth his delight feedeth himself but with wind, whereof be he never so full, he hath little substance therein. And many times shall he much deceive himself. For he shall ween that many praise him, that never speak word of him; and they that do, say yet much less than he weeneth, and far more seldom, too. For they spend not all the day (he may be sure) in talking of him alone. And whoso commends him most, will yet, I ween, in every four and twenty hours, wink and forget him once. Besides this, that while one talketh well of him in one place, another sitteth and sayeth as shrewdly of him in another. And finally some that most praise him in his presence behind his back mock him as fast and loud laugh him to scorn, and sometimes slyly to his face, too. And yet are there some fools so fed with this fond fantasy of fame that they rejoice and glory to think how they be continually praised all about, as though the world did nothing else day or night but ever sit and sing, *Sanctus, Sanctus, Sanctus,* upon them."

There is much precious ore of this kind in the *Dialogue of Comfort* for the literary student, if he will take the trifling amount of patience required for the first few pages to become accustomed to the occasional archaisms and labored constructions inseparable from prose finding its literary wings for the first time. As it is, the prose of More is hardly more archaic and certainly less awkward and floundering than the prose of Milton, who enjoyed the advantages of a most extraordinary century's growth and development to improve upon the style of his predecessor. It is futile to conjecture why an age, which reprints Ascham and Fuller for the use of young students of our early prose, should ignore so completely the vastly superior merits of Sir Thomas More.

The attention of Catholic teachers and publishers is respectfully directed to the *Dialogue of Comfort* as a promising field of enterprise.[1] Besides its value as a literary monument, it is full of bright little side lights on English life of the fifteenth century: it should stimulate historical curiosity and research. Whether the reader is looking for literature or history or prudent direction in the spiritual life, he will find the *Dialogue* a treasure. It will bring him into close communion with one of the great men of all time. And this is the surest and, it is commonly conceded, the only test of a classic.

---

[1]The *Dialogue of Comfort* is published in the popular "Everyman's Library." It occupies the second portion of the volume entitled *Utopia.*

SIR THOMAS MORE: THE HAPPY WARRIOR

IT is rumored that we shall witness before long the canonization of Blessed Thomas More. In that event, interest in the great Lord Chancellor of England will be stimulated everywhere throughout the Catholic world. Although Sir Thomas More has not been given deserved recognition in literary traditions very decidedly Protestant, still a fairly large body of literature by him and about him waits patiently to come to the surface in the sifting processes of time. Thomas More died about thirty years before Shakespeare was born, and probably, of none of the men who made that century glorious in history, is there a more authentic and detailed record than his. When it has received due attention from Catholic readers, the logical result ought to be an increase of faith and fervor.

In a general revival of interest in Thomas More it might be a rather fascinating exercise to study a great English poem in the light of his life. There is no external evidence, I suppose, for believing that Wordsworth had Thomas More in mind, when he wrote "The Happy Warrior." The poet most probably gathered suggestions of moral excellence from among his contemporaries and blended them into a picture of an ideal man. It is an austerely beautiful picture. The "Happy Warrior" is perhaps the highest flight of Wordsworth's moral fervor; it is certainly one of the few great poems in which genius does worthy homage to virtue. And it is somewhat startling to discover in this noble portrait of a man the living likeness of Thomas More.

Wordsworth could hardly have been more precise and definite in his details had he been consciously trying to distil More's life into a poem. In the long gallery of English celebrities, no one remotely approaches More to serve as an identifiable original for the portrait done by Wordsworth. The poem is an excellent commentary on More's life; and More's life is a striking illustration of the poem, actually clearing up some of the lines which might else be vague or obscure.

"Who is the Happy Warrior?" the poet begins. He undertakes to describe him, declaring, first, that it is he

> Whose high endeavors are an inward light
> That makes the path before him always bright;
> Who, with a natural instinct to discern
> What knowledge can perform, is diligent to learn;
> Abides by this resolve, and stops not there,
> But makes his moral being his prime care.

More, the light-hearted master of quip and jest, creating friendship and affection wherever he passed; More, the student, the scholar, the writer, admired of the great Erasmus; More, the stern ascetic—the three couplets could hardly be more explicit as a general outline of More's character.

Who, doomed to go in company with pain,
And fear, and bloodshed, miserable train,
Turns his necessity to glorious gain.

Read what More wrote to Meg, his favorite child, from the Tower, that gloomy bastile, the dark anteroom of the scaffold: "Surely, Meg, a fainter heart than thy frail father hath thou canst not have. . . . And verily, my dear daughter, in this is my great comfort, that albeit I am almost afraid of a filip, yet in all the agonies that I have had, I thank the mighty mercy of God, I never in my mind intend to consent to anything against my conscience." This is the only way hard necessity can be transmuted into glorious gain.

Practical man of affairs though he was, More was always the scholarly lover of seclusion and quiet, disliking turmoil, and sensitive to "pain and fear and bloodshed." His fine nature shrank from coming to issue with the crude forces of a brutal world that challenged his spiritual aspirations. But he never failed to meet the challenge promptly and boldly. And he was never betrayed into the tragic pose by his fears. He was the only man in England who saw the black cloud of schism when it was still a faint speck on the far horizon of a summer day. The keen foresight undoubtedly helped him to fortify his soul against the evil day. But it must also have filled his heart with the specters of a great fear. One thing it could not do, and that is depress his spirits.

"I thank our Lord, son," he said one day to Roper,

who had just enjoyed the pleasing experience of seeing the king call at More's home and walk back and forth in the garden with his arm around More's neck, "I thank our Lord I find his Grace my very good lord indeed, and I believe he does as singularly favor me as any subject within his realm; howbeit, son Roper, I may tell thee, I have no cause to be proud thereof, for if my head would win him a castle in France, it should not fail to go." It is clear More's gayety did not rest upon carefully fostered illusions. He knew how to dispel the shadows of coming events with the gentle radiance of humor and a playful and somewhat quizzical wit. The slower members of his family were sometimes puzzled and vexed by it; and it led the Protestant bishop Burnet later to declare very unintelligently that More was a trifler.

> But who, if he be called upon to face
> Some awful moment to which Heaven has joined
> Great issues, good or bad for human kind,
> Is happy as a lover, and attired
> With sudden brightness, like a man inspired;
> And through the heart of conflict keeps the law
> In calmness made, and sees what he foresaw.

And is there anywhere in history a more convincing instance of disinterestedness in high office? Honors fell thick upon Thomas More; but his perfect detachment kept him unshackled by the insidious curbs they impose on a free spirit. He was unimaginably above intrigue and petty politics. He was a man, if ever there was one,

> Who, if he rise to stations of command,
> Rises by open means; and there will stand
> On honorable terms, or else retire,
> And in himself possess his own desire.
> And therefore does not stoop, nor lie in wait
> For wealth and honors or for worldly state;
> Whom they must follow; on whose head must fall
> Like showers of manna, if they come at all.

Political office and honors at court never carried More away from his old friends or his old interests. No king or noble ever displaced his darling Erasmus. The homely offices of religion remained always matters of prime importance. He continued to spend the early morning hours in prayer, sing in the parish choir, and march on foot in religious processions, to the great scandal of those who deemed such gear unbecoming to the Lord High Chancellor of a great realm. When at last the storm broke upon the Church in England, the fact that he was the foremost, if not the only, champion of Catholic theology against a horde of heretics, affords proof that he had been applying himself diligently to the study of religion as well as to its practice.

It is incredible, but too strongly supported by evidence to be denied, that in all his divergent and exacting interests he was always the center of life of a large and energetic household. He imposed on his family a daily régime almost monastic in its rigors; but contrived, with a measure of success that only a genius in tact and social arts can command, to make his wishes not merely acceptable, but actually delightful and charming. Eras-

mus spread the fame of that happy home all over
Europe.

> He who, though thus imbued as with a sense
> And faculty for storm and turbulence,
> Is yet a soul whose master-bias leans
> To housefelt pleasures and to gentle scenes,
> Sweet images which, wheresoe'er he be,
> Are at his heart; and such fidelity
> It is his darling passion to approve,
> More brave for this that he hath more to love.

It is not, be it noted, a common trait of men to be
more brave, the more they have to love. The thought
of dear ones can make a brave man flinch in the supreme
trial.

Surely one of the most beautiful and touching passages in history must be the following. Roper is telling
how Meg met her father for the last time on his way
back to the Tower after his sentence of death in West-
minster Hall. She waited for him in the crowds on the
Tower wharf.

"There tarrying his coming, as soon as she saw him
after his blessing upon her knees reverently received,
she, hastening toward him, without consideration or care
of herself, pressing in among the midst of the throng
and company of the guard, that with halberts and bills
were around about him, hastily ran to him, and there
openly in sight of them all embraced him and took
him about the neck and kissed him. Who, well liking
her most natural and daughterly affection towards him,
gave her his fatherly blessing, and many godly words

of comfort besides. From whom after she was departed, she, not satisfied with the former sight of her dear father, and like one that had forgotten herself, being all ravished with the entire love of her dear father, having respect neither to herself nor to the press of people and multitude that were there about him, suddenly turned back again, ran to him as before, took him about the neck, and divers times kissed him most lovingly, and at last, with a full and heavy heart, was fain to depart from him."

This was the girl whose Latin style and knowledge of Greek won the praise of Erasmus; a spirited and affectionate girl whom any father might well find it a separate agony to part from in a final renunciation. She, with her mother, had tried to persuade her father to comply with the king's wishes and to do only what (alas!) "almost every abbess, abbot, and bishop in the country" had done. It is impossible to blame her. When the shepherds go astray, the flocks will be confused. Meg caught at the only straws she saw in a desperate effort to save a dear life. But what a cruel strain upon the fortitude of her father!

> Whom neither shape of danger can dismay,
> Nor thought of tender happiness betray.

Thomas More had passed more than a year in his Tower dungeon before he was formally found guilty of treason and executed. His delicate constitution suffered painfully in those dark, damp quarters. But his lively spirits knew no quenching. He wrote a cheerful book *On Consolation in Adversity* in the intervals of prayer, and brightened with witty and humorous observations the infamous record of his savage undoing. To the end, he was as always the Happy Warrior,

> Who, whether praise of him must walk the earth
> Forever, and to noble deeds give birth,
> Or he must fall to sleep without his fame
> And leave a dead unprofitable name,
> Finds comfort in himself and in his cause,
> And, while the mortal mist is gathering, draws
> His breath in confidence of Heaven's applause,
> This is the Happy Warrior; this is he
> Whom every man in arms should wish to be.

SOME LETTERS OF JOYCE KILMER

THE *Month* for May, 1917, contains a glowing, yet judicious, appreciation of the poetry of Joyce Kilmer by Mr. Hugh Anthony Allen. The bright little essay ends on a note of prophecy: "Over the shoulders of this green old world is rising the dawn of better things in literature and life. And Kilmer is the blithe herald of their coming." These are brave words. In July of the following year Joyce Kilmer, acting as observer for the leading battalion of his regiment, was killed in action near the Ourcq.

Joyce Kilmer was the most distinguished American soldier to fall in the late war. Two volumes, containing a selection from his poems, essays, and letters, together with a brilliantly written memoir by Mr. Robert Cortes Holliday, appeared a few months after his death, and were among the best-selling books of the season. It was not a flash in the pan. Kilmer was so wholly and so intensely Catholic that his religion showed through nearly everything that he wrote. It is not surprising, therefore, that he is still a popular author among American Catholics, especially, I am glad to say, in our schools and colleges. One might suppose that what commends him to Catholic readers would injure him elsewhere. I do not know whether it is a triumph of his personality or his art, or of both together, that, with what may be described as a flaunting and triumphant Catholicism, Kilmer has always been able to attract the general reader. That the American public had not grown tired of him six years after his death was disclosed in a poll to determine the best ten books published since 1900, conducted in 1924 by the *International Book Review*, of New York. Ballots were cast for 1,201 authors and 2,164 different books. The prevalent type among the voters may be conjectured from the fact that Mr. Wells' *Outline of History* stood highest in the poll. A list of the next 167 titles was published, the last in the column being Woodrow Wilson's *A History of the American People*. Francis Thompson's *Poems*, I am sorry to say, ranked only 158 in the list; while such popular writers as Mr. W. L. George, and Mr. Frank Swinnerton failed to come within the first hundred. Joyce Kilmer's name was fifty-fourth.

It is needless, perhaps, to state that I attach no conclusive significance to the value of this evidence in testimony of literary worth. But I think it records a remarkable phenomenon. It would seem to indicate that, after six years two volumes of poems, essays, and letters, of a strongly Catholic tone, were still popular in the English language.

This may be surprising information to English Catholic readers. When the news of Kilmer's death appeared, it was probably Mr. Gilbert K. Chesterton who wrote in the *New Witness:* "Multitudes of friends on both sides of the Atlantic, as well as many who have never seen his face, will learn with very real and poignant grief of the death in battle of Joyce Kilmer. Of his remarkable power as a poet we have no need to remind our readers." I should like to believe that Joyce Kilmer is known to multitudes on the Irish and English side of the Atlantic. It would mean that a very salutary leaven was working in the mass of contemporary reading matter. And, especially, it would mean that young Catholic writers had a gracious example to inspire them in the cultivation of the dangerous arts of beauty.

The union of piety and artistic preoccupations is as happy as it is rare. In the belief that it is a kind of concurrence which, as the world goes, attracts attention, and is of special interest to Catholics, I venture to give some extracts from his letters which throw light upon the spirit pervading Joyce Kilmer's life and work. Most of these extracts do not appear in the two volumes prepared by Mr. Holliday.

The letters, from which I quote, cover about six years. They were busy years. Kilmer was only a little over thirty when he was killed. He had married in 1906, the year of his graduation from Columbia University, on little more than a brave confidence in his future. He taught Latin in Morristown for a year and then went to New York where he was one of the editors of Funk and Wagnall's *Standard Dictionary* for three years.

Since I wrote to you last, I have left the employ of Funk and Wagnall's. . . . My present occupation is that of assistant editor of *The Churchman*, an Anglican weekly paper. It is a church newspaper, with some literary features. I am glad to say that we hope to print some of Miss Guiney's poems this winter. . . . Your remarks, in your last letter, on the fact that many of our most famous writers today are anti-Christian, are certainly justified. Still, do you not think that a reaction is coming? Already we have Chesterton, and Belloc, and Bazin, and Miss Guiney, and Father Vincent McNabb, and a number of other brilliant writers who, not as theologians but purely as literary artists, express a fine and wholesome faith. People are beginning to tire of cheap eroticism and "realism" and similar absurdities. But the flood of putrid literature still pours from the presses. Here on my desk as I write lies *The* ————, by one X. He is a vulgarian and a liar; his book is written in wretched English; it is full of grotesque and obvious falsities—and it is in its third edition. I have read the book through, and I am so sick of the fellow's cheap blasphemies that I cannot quiet myself enough to review it in printable words. I understand now thoroughly the custom of having books burned by the common hangman. It was not necessarily because the books were dangerous, or likely to lead people astray—it was just because they were essentially evil, things to be put out of the way. Well, we can't have *The* ———— burned, but you must pray for me to get words fiery enough to consume the book utterly when I review it.

Kilmer after some months left the staff of *The Churchman* and plunged into the journalism of Broadway. He began to lead a very active life, filling three or four positions on newspapers and weeklies, writing poems and articles—he had already published a volume of poems which was well received by critics—often using for his work the greater part of the nights after "commuting" to the little outlying town where he had established his home. One of his children was stricken with infantile paralysis. Months of anxiety were passed by the busy wage earner and his wife. Then the news came of their entrance into the Church. I may mention that his wife, Aline Kilmer, is widely known as a poet of fine and delicate distinction. Shortly after his conversion he writes:

The Church refuses to live up to its reputation. In the first place, no one ever tried to proselytize me. I hung on the edge, but my Catholic friends would not push. I had to jump. And now that I am in, the Church still refuses to live up to its reputation. I was warned that I would be shocked by the begging of the parish clergy. I wish I could find a real begging priest. My pastor begs not half enough. Seriously, I think the Church is slandered more by educated Catholic laymen than by Protestants. Even when I was a Protestant, I was pained by some things that Catholics of my acquaintance said about the Church. Surely there should be reticence about family scandals.

Of course you understand my conversion. I am beginning to understand it. I believed in the Catholic position, the Catholic view of ethics and æsthetics, for a long time. But I wanted something not intellectual, some conviction not mental—in fact, I wanted faith. Just off Broadway, on the way from the Hudson Tube Station to the *Times* Building, there is a church, called the Church of the Holy Innocents. Since it is in the heart of the Tenderloin, this name is strangely appropriate—for there surely is need of youth and innocence. Well, every morning for months I stopped on my way to the office and prayed in this church for faith. When faith did come, it came, I think, by way of my little paralyzed daughter. Her lifeless hands led me; I think her tiny still feet know beautiful paths. You understand this, and it gives me a selfish pleasure to write it down.

In another letter about this time:

My wife and I are very comfortable now that we are Catholics. I think we rather disappointed the priest who received us by not showing any emotion during the ceremony. But our chief sensation is simply comfort—we feel that we are where we belong, and it's a very pleasant feeling.

And a little later on:

I need some stricter discipline, I think, and it's hard to get it. I enjoy my confessor's direction very much; he is a fine old Irishman with no nonsense about him. But I need to be called a fool, I need to have some of the conceit and sophistication knocked out of me. I suppose you think this is "enthusiasm"—that much-heralded danger of converts. Perhaps it is, but I don't think so. I know I'm glad I live two miles from the church, because it's excellent for a lazy person like myself to be made to exert himself for religion. And I wish I had a stern medieval confessor—the sort one reads about in anti-Catholic books—who would inflict real penances. The saying of Hail Marys and Our Fathers is no penance, it's a delight.

After this letter the discerning reader will not have to be informed that Kilmer had a conscience peculiarly delicate without being unduly scrupulous. I had frequent occasions of surprise over the sensitiveness of conscience which he preserved in occupations popularly supposed to destroy spiritual refinements. He was a daily communicant. One evening during a visit he told me that he had been reading that day an article which appeared on the first page of a reputable newspaper. He began to realize that he should not continue reading, and he cast the paper aside; but he was not sure whether he had acted promptly enough, and might he receive in the morning? Although very substantial and cheerful in appearance, he impressed everyone with a sense of purity and spirituality. Mr. Richard Le Gallienne noted this fact in an article shortly after Kilmer's death: he ends a long description of his first meeting with Kilmer with these words: "I must not omit from my impression the feeling of an unaccustomed contact with vigorous purity, again masculine, not feminine, purity."

To go back to letters.

Did I tell you my confessor sent me to Msgr. Mooney (Vicar-General of the Diocese) to get permission to read anti-religious books and magazines? I am obliged to read them in my work, you know. Msgr. Mooney told me to go ahead and read them if I had to.

A schoolroom essay on his poems sent to him from a convent drew the following acknowledgment:

Your generous and well-phrased appreciation has made me happy, and I am grateful. I hope and pray that I may never write anything unworthy to be read by you.

Joyce Kilmer found genuine pleasure, I think, in giving readings and lectures. The popular demand for them grew every year, and he found in them recreation and a welcome means of eking out an income for an increasing family. He enjoyed Catholic audiences; but, in starting out as a Catholic lecturer, certain reluctances had to be overcome.

I'll probably lecture before Catholic organizations as well as secular ones, but I don't want to for reasons you will understand. In the first place, I don't want in any way to make money out of my religion, to seem to be a "professional Catholic." In the second place, I have delight chiefly in talking veiled Catholicism to non-Catholics, in humbly endeavoring to be an apostle to Bohemia. For instance, I'd rather smash an evil book by X. in *The Times* than praise a good book in *America*. I have no real message for Catholics; I have Catholicism's message to modern pagans. So I want to lecture chiefly to pagans.

In the summer of 1916 he met with an accident on the railway at the little country station near his home:

It may interest you to know that I had received the Blessed Sacrament half an hour before the train struck me, and that to this fact I attribute my escape from death—since at the place where I was struck several men have been killed, being thrown forward and under the wheels, instead of (as I was) to one side.

His practice of daily Communion made it necessary to go into New York without his breakfast and to have his morning coffee at a restaurant. He was living in Mahwah, New Jersey, two hours by rail from New York. He wore his piety without heroics:

Terribly pious, I am. You won't know me when you see me. Probably I'll sit around and lecture you all the time. Daily communicant and all that sort of thing. And I find all other daily communicants are funny old women with disreputable bonnets and two clanking rosaries apiece. They clatter up to the rail leaning on canes and pray audibly.

He was always ready to improve the frequent opportunities which came to him of urging the claims of Catholic literary merit.

By the way, it may interest you to know of an experience I had recently with Warner's Library of the World's Best Literature. This is, as you undoubtedly are aware, a monumental work founded by the late Charles Dudley Warner. It is supposed to represent adequately all the world's greatest writers, and the biographical and critical articles are supposed to be authoritative. The list of editors is most imposing, and when I was asked to contribute to the revised edition articles on Cawein, Masefield, and Moody, I was much pleased. Out of curiosity, I asked the editor who was writing the article on Francis Thompson. To my amazement I found he had not thought of including Thompson! I am glad to say that I succeeded in persuading him to include an article on Thompson. I am writing it and selecting four or five pages of extracts from Thompson to accompany it. Do you think that some of Thompson's prose should be included, or only his verse?

In a letter, dated May 19th, 1917, he writes:

I resigned from the Officer's Reserve Training Corps and enlisted in the Seventh Regiment, National Guard, New York, as a private.

Joyce Kilmer has been the object of some disapproval for taking this step. He had a wife and five children depending upon him for their support, and there was no urgency for a sacrifice which involved others as well as himself. And, as afterward transpired, once in the army and at the front he deliberately sought the most perilous employments. My own explanation, which space will not permit amplifying, is that Joyce Kilmer acted at this time from spiritual motives at least as much as from patriotic motives. As for his family, he had received what seemed to be the most reliable assurances that they would be provided for in the event of his death. If misunderstanding on this score developed afterward, he could not possibly have foreseen it.

In the letter announcing his enlistment, after telling about certain courtesies he had received, he proceeds:

On the whole I'm too well treated—it's likely to turn my head. That's why it's good for me to be a private and be bossed around by a young snip of an officer I wouldn't hire as an office boy. Every drill night I have about 300 exercises in humility—every time the sergeant says, "Get your belly in!" "Hold up your head!" "Say, that's a gun you're carrying, not a hod!"

He seldom thereafter referred in his letters to the hardships of his soldier life. He obtained a transfer from the Seventh to the Sixty-Ninth, the Irish Regiment of New York, principally because it had a Catholic chaplain and was predominantly Catholic and Irish, a combination which always attracted him. His regiment was a part of the Rainbow Division which was one of the earliest to go overseas. On the eve of its departure, his favorite child, the crippled Rose, died, and another child was born. It was a difficult time. He refers to the "eight hours a day of violent physical exercise (most deadening to the brain, a useful anodyne to me, coming as it did after my grief)," and that is all one hears of the sordid horrors of war, bad enough during the regiment's first winter in France. His letters were for the most part full of good humor and high spirits. The last lines of a short poem sent home from the front tells us much:

> Lord, Thou didst suffer more for me
> Than all the hosts of land and sea.
> So let me render back again
> This millionth of Thy gift. Amen.

Even if it be granted that the radiant presence of Joyce Kilmer is still a vivid memory, influencing those who knew him to set too high a value upon his literary work, it is nevertheless true that his writings disclose an extraordinary personality in which amiable human qualities, literary activity and ambition, and high natural virtues, were fused with a scrupulously exact Catholic and supernatural life and faith. This alone should keep him from dropping into oblivion among Catholics. It is not often that the febrile pursuits of journalism and literature produce a popular writer who can be cited as an example and an inspiration in the great and the small Catholic fidelities. These words, written in one of his last letters to his wife and appearing in the two-volume work to which reference has been made, might well be framed and hung on the wall wherever writing talent is laboring for mastery in the art of expression:

If what you write does not clearly praise the Lord and His saints and angels, let it praise such types of heaven as we know in our life —God knows they are numerous enough. I can honestly offer *Trees* and *Main Street* [the titles of the two volumes of poems which he published after he had become a Catholic] to Our Lady, and ask her to present them, as the faithful work of her poor and unskilled craftsman, to her Son. I hope to be able to do it with everything I write hereafter—and to be able to do this is to be a good poet.

THE PAGANISM OF MR. YEATS

IT IS more than twenty years since I listened to Mr. William Butler Yeats explaining to a large American audience his gospel of the beautiful. A tall, graceful form; a countenance of winning intelligence, stamped with the preoccupied and pathetic ardors of the visionary; dark hair parted at the side and allowed to fall carelessly in a heavy mass over a high forehead; a voice that paid no attention to itself, so engrossed was it with ideas, but pleasing withal; gestures of natural courtesy, and the aura of a great reputation —such external recommendations as these were not lost upon the poet's audience. He seemed like a young god of the Greeks, Hyperion, as it were, in evening dress.

The suggestion of a Greek god was carried out in the tenor of his speech. He presented himself to us as a leader in a national movement. The modern spirit of commercialism, he said, was destroying the beauty and happiness of the world. It was rampant in England, and had penetrated Irish life. He had consecrated all his powers to restore to his native land the antique reverence and heroic gesture of its pagan gods, its fighting men and milk-white valorous women of pre-Christian days. Ireland was to be redeemed from its bondage to England and the modern spirit of commercialism by a revival of popular belief in fairies. The folklore of the people on the western coast of Ireland, where English tradition had made least headway, was saturated with poetry of an unearthly loveliness, which would regenerate decadent Ireland.

The eloquent young lecturer kept in touch with his hard-headed American audience by admitting that the Gaelic revival, as it was outlined by him, was most probably a movement of defeat. But he won all hearts by the fervor of his declaration that a true man wrought according to his ideals, never stopping to calculate chances or to ask whether defeat or success awaited the end of his day's work. It was a most unworldly attitude: and there are few persons so worldly as not to enjoy the spectacle of other-worldliness, especially when it is invested with the charm of poetry and the accents of a comely and youthful dreamer.

I can recall the puzzled state of my feelings at the time. The lecturer's other world was different from mine. His was a world of shadowy and baleful forms and voices, evoked from the glooms of night and the terrors and tendernesses of winds and waves and lonely mountain glades. Mine was a world of spiritual realities, divinely gracious, as actual to me as the body I wore, and far more precious. This world of mine, which has been called the Kingdom of Heaven, had supplanted that world of his at infinite cost, and had inspired heroisms of service and sacrifice in order to carry light and hope and gladness to that whilom world which the Irish poet depicted in such attractive colors. He cheapened everything that I held sacred and passing fair, and glorified a system of life and conduct, which, whatever may be said about the externals of its pageantry, harbored horror and corruption at its heart. Nowhere was my world so quickly and firmly and gratefully established in the hearts of the people as in the land of his birth, where it has endured through centuries of prosperity at first, and then of unparalleled trials, as a most potent spiritual force at the service of all mankind. The young poet seemed actually to resent the completeness of the Christian conquest of his native land. There was an unaccustomed note of stridency in his voice when he asserted that his movement would brook no dictation from the pulpits of his country.

And yet one could not find it in his heart to dislike the young poet who was so obviously sincere in advocating a lost cause, even though it was the lost cause of all the spirits of darkness. I could only sit and wonder and make surmises about the formation of mind, the prejudice, the habits, the association and studies and temper of soul, which could so blind a man of high intelligence to the moral and spiritual beauty of Christianity as to lead him to express a deliberate preference, on ethical as well as æsthetic grounds, for the weird paganisms of the past. If there are any good reasons for Matthew Arnold's definition of poetry, namely, that it is a criticism of life, what are we to think of poetry which declares that paganism is a more desirable thing than Christianity? Rationalism merely registers a broad fact at its minimum valuation when it tells us through one of its favorite historians: "It was reserved for Christianity to present to the world an ideal character, which through all the changes of eighteen centuries has inspired the hearts of men with an impassioned love; has shown itself capable of acting on all ages, nations, temperaments, and conditions; has been not only the highest pattern of virtue, but the strongest incentive to its practice, and has exercised so deep an influence that it may be truly said that the simple record of three short years of active life has done more to regenerate and to soften mankind, than all the disquisitions of philosophers, and all the exhortations of moralists." And it might be added without fear of contradiction, "than all poems ancient and modern."

I could not help concluding, after hearing Mr. Yeats explain the principles of his art, that he was living strangely apart from the great streams of humanity. His points of contact with life, especially in his native land, were its fancies and extravagances rather than its realities. Subsequent confirmation was not lacking in certain essays, in which the Irish poet writes about fairies in a vein of religious reverence and belief, and in casual allusions met with in the publication of his friends where they refer to him as "Willie" Yeats in a tone of amused indulgence, as if he were hopelessly committed to eccentricities of thought.

I need not say that many men prefer paganism to Christianity for worse reasons than an obstinately unpractical turn of mind. Perhaps this is the consideration which procures for Mr. Yeats a kindly tolerance from people who find neopaganism a bore and a nuisance. He seems so simple and honest in the weaving of his filmy lacework of pale dreams that one pities him for finding Christianity "lower than the heart's desire." One has to understand Mr. Yeats; his is the winsome willfulness of infancy; concessions must be made to peculiarities of mind out of the common run; if he hurts us with his pretty arrows, he does it as a child does it, that is, in the least offensive of all possible modes of assault.

But great poetry cannot spring from such a soil. Sanity and sobriety of judgment on the large issues of life are still, and always have been, the marks of major poets and prose-writers. "I'd rather be a kitten and cry, Mew! than write the best poetry in the world on condition of laying aside common sense in the ordinary transactions and business of the world." It is probable Sir Walter Scott knew very well that great poetry could never be written on such a condition; but his words serve to illustrate the attitude of genius of the highest rank in the relationship of art to life.

It is unfortunate for the cause of poetry that a man of Mr. Yeats's fervor and workmanship should have become early and permanently obsessed by an impossible idea. "The attempt to revive an ancient myth—as distinguished from an ancient story of human life—however alluring, however illustrated by poets of genius, seems to me," says that acute critic of poetry, Francis T. Palgrave, "essentially impossible. It is for the details, not for the whole, that we read *Hyperion,* or *Prometheus Unbound,* or the German *Iphigenia.* Like the great majority of post-classical verse in classical languages, those modern myths are but exercises on a splendid scale." The Gaelic revival became for Mr. Yeats nothing else than precisely that, namely, an endeavor to resuscitate a dead past, and to furnish forth out of its outworn emotions and primitive religious experiences food and raiment for modern needs. Mr. Yeats has succeeded in composing some graceful academic exercises; nothing more. With doubts about the vital actuality of his method, he has employed a loose symbolism to establish contact with the world of living men; but the device can hardly be said to have succeeded in winning for his verse attention more serious than that which we pay to mere brilliant exercises of an accomplished artist. Mr. Yeats has wasted excellent poetic capacity in becoming a minor poet, engaged in the gentle but ineffectual labor of rescuing a remote twilight and an ancient darkness from the floods of splendor in which St. Patrick's flaming sword engulfed them.

If anyone wishes to study the sterility of the sources to which Mr. Yeats has gone for inspiration, he will discover a striking object-lesson in the poet's published volume of selected poems.[1] They are conveniently divided for such a study into chronological periods. If we confine ourselves to the lyrics, which are more characteristic of Mr. Yeats's genius than his dramatic pieces and contain the flower of his achievement, we shall find a curiously progressive deterioration in his work. The earliest group of poems is dated 1885–1892, and contains such favorites as "The Lake Isle of Innisfree," "The Fiddler of Dooney," and "The Ballad of Father Gilligan." Here are the new and entrancing magic and music which charmed us years ago and sharpened the edge of expectation. Alas, for youthful promise!

The young poet sang from the peak of his excellence. He has never surpassed these little miracles of rare Celtic rapture: their secret has escaped the bewildered singer, and his song since then has been a groping effort, successful at ever lengthening intervals, to recover that first fine careless rapture. There are notes of sadness and failure in the later poems of the period between 1904 and 1919, and it is rather poignant to read, in one of the last poems in the collection,

> I have no speech but symbol, the pagan speech I made
> Amid the dreams of youth.

If there is need of a crowning proof of the falseness and futility of the trail which Mr. Yeats has been following, it can be found in the rather astounding absence, in these later poems, of any sign of interest in the recent

---

[1]*Selected Poems*, by William Butler Yeats (New York: The Macmillan Co.).

stirring history of his country. When he was young he declared his pagan creed, with all the bold confidence of youth, in his "To Ireland in the Coming Times," turning his back on the traditional sanctities of his land and sighing ecstatically,

> Ah, faeries, dancing under the moon,
> A Druid land, a Druid tune!

and he promises himself, despite his recusancy, a secure place among the patriot bards of Irish history:

> Nor may I less be counted one
> With Davis, Mangan, Ferguson.

How pitiful sounds this young boast in the presence of the mature performance! The little red Rose was plunged in its bath of heroic blood, and the deeds of Cuchulainn and all the chariot-chiefs and kings of Ulster were outdone, while cities flamed and tumbled, and all the world looked on in wonder; and Mr. Yeats can find nothing to inspire a song except some cryptic discontent of his own at the course of events. I know nothing whatever concerning the political ideas of Mr. Yeats during these years; but I gather from these poems that he was out of sympathy with the men who cast life and liberty and possessions into the scales in a supreme conflict for their country's freedom. If I am correct in my surmise, it is a sinister commentary on the uselessness of a false intellectualism in any practical crisis. I do not deny the sincerity and fervor of Mr. Yeats's patriotism. It is through no immediate fault of his that the great dawn of his dreams should break at long last and find him listless. The fault is to be traced back to that remote day when he so far departed from realities as to scorn the living Faith which has been the mainstay of his people through trials in which pretty Druid fancies would be insults if they were offered as hopes or alleviations.

The strange irony of the situation lies in the fact that the men who blew the smoldering dreams of Ireland into the white flame of Easter Week and perished in it with exultation, caught much of their enthusiasm from Mr. Yeats's own sources. The two Pearses, Padraic and William, Thomas MacDonagh and Joseph Plunkett, not to mention others, drew inspiration and instruction from the fine idealism of old Celtic legends of early paganism. The fire which Mr. Yeats was so prominent in kindling, gave them warmth at the supreme moment, but could impart no life-giving heat to himself. For the Irish poet's theory of life is a paralyzing thing. The nature-worship of Celtic paganism, which so captivates him, contains no concepts of right or wrong, duty or obligation. "No thought of Calvary," he makes one of the characters say in "The Land of Heart's Desire," "troubled the morning stars in their first song." It is hard for the ordinary Christian to see why the thought of Calvary should cause trouble, rather than great love and hope, to anyone: but, of course, the poet is correct. Stars and mountains and winds and similar objects of nature are never troubled by any thoughts whatever.

The irresponsible freedom of the wild things of nature fascinates the poet. The trouble of living rationally, of thinking and obeying and performing duty, is distasteful to him. Any religion which emphasizes the responsibility of the individual, and presents truth with a corollary of precept—as the Catholic religion does—fatigues and disgusts Mr. Yeats. And so we have lyrics like the following, in which he draws his robe about him and withdraws disdainfully from the human world, as from a lower world than the mindless world which he loves:

> Outworn heart, in a time outworn,
> Come clear of the nets of wrong and right;
> Laugh, heart, again in the gray twilight,
> Sigh, heart, again in the dew of the morn.
>
> Your mother Eire is always young,
> Dew ever shining and twilight gray;
> Though hope fall from you and love decay,
> Burning in fires of a slanderous tongue.
>
> Come, heart, where hill is heaped upon hill:
> For there the mystical brotherhood
> Of sun and moon and hollow and wood
> And river and stream work out their will;
>
> And God stands winding His lonely horn,
> And time and the world are ever in flight;
> And love is less kind than the gray twilight,
> And hope is less dear than the dew of the morn.

As the beautiful expression of a common mood, these verses can be accorded due admiration. Wordsworth has done it better in a famous sonnet, though he was not "a pagan suckled in a creed outworn." As an expression of a philosophy of life it is fatuous and futile.

Padraic Pearse's philosophy was different, and can be inferred from the verses which he could write for his mother while he was waiting for the firing squad:

> Dear Mary, thou who saw thy first-born Son
> Go forth to die amidst the scorn of men,
> Receive my first-born son into thy arms
> Who also goeth forth to die for men;
> And keep him by thee till I come for him.
> Dear Mary, I have shared thy sorrows,
> And soon shall share thy joys.

Thomas MacDonagh passed the hours between the time his sister, a nun, left his cell and the moment of execution, kneeling before his crucifix. These leaders in a desperate chance all went to Confession and Holy Communion as a preparation for fighting and dying. Michael Mallen, we read, "prayed into the very rifles of the men who shot him, and his last words were: 'Lord Jesus, receive my spirit!'" And in his last letter to his wife we find, among other instructions, the following: "If you can, I would like you to dedicate Una to the service of God, and also Joseph. Do this if you can, and pray our Divine Lord that it may be so. . . . Una, my little one, be a nun. Joseph, my little man, be a priest if you can."

Mr. Yeats's "September, 1913," inclines us to suspect that his view of facts like these is derisory and contemptuous:

What need you, being come to sense,
But fumble in a greasy till
And add the half pence to the pence
And prayer to shivering prayer, until
You have dried the marrow from the bone;
For men were born to pray and save:
Romantic Ireland's dead and gone,
It's with O'Leary in the grave.

Yet they were of a different kind
The names that stilled your childish play,
They have gone about the world like wind,
But little time had they to pray
For whom the hangman's rope was spun,
And what, God help us, could they save:
Romantic Ireland's dead and gone,
It's with O'Leary in the grave.

Was it for this the wild geese spread
The gray wing upon every tide;
For this that all that blood was shed,
For this Edward Fitzgerald died,
And Robert Emmet and Wolfe Tone,
All that delirium of the brave?
Romantic Ireland's dead and gone,
It's with O'Leary in the grave.

Yet could we turn the years again,
And call those exiles as they were,
In all their loneliness and pain
You'd cry "some woman's yellow hair
Has maddened every mother's son":
They weighed so lightly what they gave;
But let them be, they're dead and gone,
They're with O'Leary in the grave.

Thus Mr. Yeats in "September, 1913." Only two years

later, there broke forth such a delirium of the brave as Mr. Yeats never dreamed. And the only men who figured prominently in the outbreak were young clerks and teachers who found time to pray, waiting for the executioner, because prayer had been a lifelong habit. As between Pearse and Mr. Yeats, there can be no doubt which Emmet would recognize as a kindred spirit. Was ever a poet's reading of his people so palpably and so quickly falsified? I am astonished that Mr. Yeats should have had the courage to include in his *Selected Poems* "September, 1913," after Easter Week, 1916.

It is a rather ungracious speculation, but one can hardly help wondering whether Mr. Yeats's lyrical inertness in the stirring events of recent years is due to the marked Christian character of the valor so epically displayed. I am certain he shares none of the blind bigotry of the sectaries of the North. But even a kindly and tolerant paganism loses patience sometimes with an inflexible creed; and we are not surprised to find the furry, soft, and charming paganism of Mr. Yeats unsheathing acerbities in a note appended to "The Countess Cathleen." At the first performance of this play in Dublin, the actors, we are told, "had to face a very vehement opposition stirred up by a politician and a newspaper, the one accusing me in a pamphlet, the other in long articles, day after day, of blasphemy because of the language of the demons or of Shemus Rua, and because I made a woman sell her soul and yet escape damnation, and of a lack of patriotism because I made

Irish men and women, who, it seems, never did such a thing, sell theirs. The politician or the newspaper persuaded some forty Catholic students to sign a protest against the play, and a Cardinal, who avowed that he had not read it, to make another, and both politician and newspaper made such obvious appeals to the audience to break the peace, that a score or so of police were sent to the theater to see that they did not. I had, however, no reason to regret the result, for the stalls, containing almost all that was distinguished in Dublin, and a gallery of artisans alike, insisted on the freedom of literature." Literature, of course, must be free, free to hurt the weakest and to desecrate the highest, even though one must sell his soul to exercise that freedom. But when I reflect that the poet, who thought it admirable for a lady to sell her soul for her country, sat in safe seclusion while the Catholic students, who denounced the nefarious transaction, were selling their lives for his country, I am again astonished at some of the inclusions in this volume of selected poems.

The frozen apathy of Mr. Yeats's muse in the high tide of his country's heroic mood can be due only to his poor understanding of the soul of Ireland. He worships beauty in the abstract, and believes that a poet should be concerned with the making of beautiful poems, regardless of moral, religious, or patriotic import. He tells us in verses which do not find a place in his selected poems that:

> When I was young
> I had not given a penny for a song
> Did not the poet sing it with such airs
> That one believed he had a sword upstairs,

and he snorts at this allegiance of poetry to any cause
whatever. In those young days, he thought he saw
beauty in a far-off paganism, whose harshnesses came
softened to him by the mists of distance, and he dedi-
cated his muse to the service of paganism with a devotion that can hardly be said to have languished much in
the interval. Now, I do not think I shall offend historical judgment in any sane quarter by saying that the
soul of Ireland, if it has worn beauty as a garment any
time these fifteen hundred years, has worn it woven of
the faith and aspiration and white purities and rubrical
sacrifices of Catholic fidelities and consecrations. How
can a poet, who seems to be organically bereft of the
power to see so prominent a reality, hope to "be counted
one with Davis, Mangan, Ferguson" in the memory of
his country and mankind?

The sad fact is that the early impulse of "The Wind
Among the Reeds" has been too tenuous and too unre-
lated with reality to survive. Mr. Yeats, having lost his
lyric voice, busies himself now with fantastic experi-
ments in drama. His "Four Plays for Dancers," appearing almost simultaneously with his volume of *Selected Poems*, offered small compensation to those who
have liked him for his singing quality. In these new

plays, he went to the old Greek theater for hints in construction, setting, and properties. It is not easy to describe the result. The vague, shadowy, formless visions of Oisin are not happy amid the precise proprieties of classic Greece. Mr. Yeats and the school of Irish poets which he has founded remind me of Lady Penelope and Lady Binks and the other fair revelers at Shaws-Castle: "Who can describe the wonders wrought by active needles and scissors, aided by thimbles and thread, upon silver gauze and sprigged muslin? Or, who can show how, if the fair nymphs of the spring did not entirely succeed in attaining the desired resemblance to heathen Greeks, they at least contrived to get rid of all similitude to sober Christians?"

THE INTOLERANT EMERSON

THIS kind of essay, I am free to confess, should not be encouraged. The *advocatus diaboli* is deservedly unpopular. But it seems to me there are extenuating circumstances which make it pardonable to enact that rôle in the canonizing processes long going on in favor of Ralph Waldo Emerson. The man has been disgracefully overpraised to the moral and intellectual scandal of several generations of Americans. Indeed, the high-power spotlights of popular worship play upon his august figure with such fierce white radiance that recusancy seems a rather harmless amusement. He has been apotheosized into a kind of abstract excellence, an immortal shade in a vague Elysium where he takes orders from nobody. Who can imagine Emerson bowing down anywhere to anybody? What damage can the pellet from an insurrectionary popgun do a divine shadow? His invulnerability almost makes him a legitimate target. A brickbat is an innocuous missile to a ghost, *par levibus ventis.*

I do not deny that Emerson has sometimes been to me a source of great delight. I have at times fallen under his spell and joined in the popular applause. But he has also induced moods of violent disgust; and, if I yield to one of them without allowing the memory of

his virtues to soften my asperity, does not he himself
urge me on in his own mellifluously unctuous manner?

Why drag about this corpse of your memory, lest you contradict
what you have stated in this or that public place? Suppose you
should contradict yourself: what then? It seems to be a rule of wisdom never to rely on your memory alone, scarcely even in arts of
pure memory, but to bring the past for judgment into the thousand-
eyed present, and live ever in a new day. In your metaphysics you
have denied personality to the Deity, yet when the devout motions of
the soul come, yield to them heart and life, though they clothe God
with shape and color. Leave your theory, as Joseph his coat in the
hands of the harlot, and flee. A foolish consistency is the hobgoblin
of little minds, adored by little statesmen and philosophers and di-
vines. With consistency a great soul has simply nothing to do. He
may as well concern himself with his shadow on the wall. Speak
what you think now in hard words and tomorrow speak what tomorrow thinks in hard words again, though it contradict everything
you said today.

These are brave words. They are a plenary indulgence, in a muddled Protestant understanding of the
phrase, for all possible unkindnesses of speech. I think
I can promise that I shall not be so coarse and untruth-
ful and malevolently disposed toward Emerson as he
has been toward me. For there were three things which
could, from his youth to his old age, disturb the serene
surface of Emerson's soul and roil it with the ugly
sludge of his hatred and contempt. Being a Catholic
was one; being an Irishman was another; and being a
Jesuit was the third. I happen to be after a fashion a
wretched coincidence of all three, and peculiarly fa-
vored by my experience in this triple character to receive

in its fullest impact the solemn fatuousness of the Concord preacher. The noble Emerson's designation for an Irishman was "a Paddy." As for the Catholic Church, with the pages of Christendom lying open before his eyes, it never occurred to this scholar of boastful magnanimity that the mightiest spiritual institution of history was anything else than a heaving mass of ignorance, superstition, corruption, and hypocrisy which continued to exist through the illiteracy of weak-minded populations and by the tricks of a crafty priesthood, of which Jesuits were particularly odious representatives.

In itself, Emerson's hostility to the Church was not so singular a phenomenon as to astonish me. A lifelong Catholic reader of English and American literatures soon comes to expect and be indifferent to rude and blundering attacks upon his dearest attachments. But there is in Emerson's inherited and more or less natural hatred of the Church a peculiarly provincial venom and fixture which one never grows quite used to. In this respect he affords the best example we know of that consistency which is the hobgoblin of little minds. We cannot recall a really great writer, since the Protestant tradition began to dominate English literature, who had not lucid intervals in his mad obsession against the Church. Sir Walter Scott, Thackeray, Ruskin, Stevenson, expressed regret for unkindnesses of pen into which the prejudices of early training and the precipitancy of youth had betrayed them. It is possible to weave a gar-

land of tributes to the beauty of Catholic sanctity and
the high moral mission of the Church out of the writings of non-Catholic poets and prose writers of eminence who enjoyed no larger opportunities of enlighten-
ment than Emerson. But no contribution for that gar-
land can be found in him. The hard-set and iron com-
press of New England Puritanism kept him from looking about. From first to last Emerson remained un-
changed in his views of the Church. This was his blind
side. And how very blind it was!

One is at a loss to know how to convey some notion
of the peculiar virulence of Emerson's fanatical de-
testation of the Catholic Church. It was not shared in
the same degree, as far as I am aware, by any contemporary American of first-rate intelligence. Hawthorne,
Holmes, Thoreau, Webster, and Poe were not such
frenzied dervishes as Emerson on the subject of the
Church. In order to make comparisons here, we should
have to search the Masonic lodges of country districts
or the isolated hamlets of the Western wilderness. A
settled invincibility of ignorance about Catholic matters, distorting vision, warping judgment, and dealing
in crude invective, is a point of resemblance, which
makes Emerson and Albert Pike curiously alike. We
can more easily forgive Pike. He cultivated no pre-
tensions to being a cosmopolitan philosopher living a
life of high thought far above all local partisanships
and the passions of the hour.

Perhaps the best way of understanding this serious

fault in Emerson's intellectual equipment is to recall that charming archbigot, George Borrow. Borrow missed all the opportunities for culture and accomplishments which Emerson enjoyed. He was a blacksmith, a pugilist, a vagrant, a friend of gypsies, a colporteur. Like many self-made men he was steeped and dyed in the definite colors of his district. He was incurably provincial in his religious ideas as well as in his manners. He accepted unquestionably all the dull and stupid lies about the Church which until recently were irresistible political weapons among the lower orders of English society. His dislike of Irishmen and Catholics and Jesuits was every bit as keen and securely lodged as Emerson's. But his genius triumphs at times over the Calvinistic fastnesses in which his lot was cast. Thus, in that fascinating account of his fantastic mission of Protestant propaganda in Spain, he writes:

However attached to his religion—and who is so attached to the Romanish creed as the Irishman?—I am convinced that not all the authority of the Pope or the Cardinals could induce him to close his doors on Luther himself, were that respectable personage at present alive and in need of food and refuge. Honor to Ireland and her "hundred thousand welcomes." Her fields have long been the greenest in the world; her daughters the fairest, her sons the bravest and most eloquent. May they never cease to be so!

The man, you see, is human, after all. He may be a violent bigot. But he is not altogether a monster. Again, when he visited the English College in Valladolid:

Of sights the most remarkable is the picture gallery which contains neither more nor less than the portraits of a variety of scholars of this house who eventually suffered martyrdom in England, in the exercise of their vocation in the angry times of the Sixth Edward and the fierce Elizabeth. Yes, in this very house where many of those pale smiling half-foreign priests were educated, who, like stealthy grimalkins, traversed green England in all directions; crept into old halls beneath umbrageous rookeries, fanning the dying embers of Popery, with no other hope nor perhaps wish than to perish disemboweled by the bloody hands of the executioner, among the yells of a rabble as bigoted as themselves: priests like Bedingfield and Garnet, and many others who have left a name in English story. Doubtless many a history, only the more wonderful for being true, could be wrought out of the archives of the English Popish seminary of Valladolid.

One does not come upon such airy open spaces in Emerson. There is something feminine and spiteful in the inveteracy of Emerson's pique at all things Catholic. It is not the quality of a great man. It belongs more properly to sewing circles of malicious tendencies. It invalidates his claims to be taken for a man of supreme genius. As a village wonder he will always be remarkable. On the large stage of the world he will look more and more diminutive as the passionate quarrels of the sixteenth century subside and the thick dust of its controversies is laid. It is the fate of all mad writers against the Catholic Church to become curiosities rather than classics.

Emerson may be described as a secularized Calvinist blessed with imagination and eloquence and eager to set the world right. His self-righteousness is appalling. He makes you sit at his feet. You can draw up to a table for high discourse with Hazlitt, and even with

Carlyle; Shakespeare and Milton speak to you as man to man. But Emerson must always climb into a very lofty pulpit and his audience must sink into very lowly pews. His Puritan ecclesiasticism continued to flourish after his Puritan creed had fallen into dissolution, as hair is said to continue growing on a dead man's head.

Emerson's homiletic solemnity, as of a Father of the Church, was a mighty weapon in his attacks on Christianity. Robert Herrick flung the manuscript of his last sermon into the faces of his sleeping congregation and went out of the church to be a poet and man of the world. Emerson took his gown and surplice with him. He was not insensible to the meek adoration served up to a popular preacher by soulful admirers. If he could not be a Christian, he was determined at least to remain a preacher. We have to pay homage to the skill and ingenuity which he exercised in carrying out his difficult purpose without shocking public opinion. The transition from Puritanism to Unitarianism was prepared for by respectable precedents. From a fashionable Unitarian preacher to a kind of glorified Ethics Society professor the distance is scarcely perceptible. And since Emerson always wore his Christian cassock, his listeners were convinced that he knew all there was to be known about the Christianity which he attacked. Here was a man from the inside, who had explored the possibilities and promises of the Christian Church and found them illusory and deceitful. They could see that he would not have turned upon Christianity if he could help it.

Did he not love it so much that he continued to wear its outward livery? Thus Emerson duped the multitude. "The fact is," Ruskin once told Gladstone, "I was brought up to the Protestant faith, and consequently know nothing of Christianity."

In Puritan surroundings it is not an unprofitable venture to give a religious coloring to a purely secular enterprise. Indeed, it is a characteristic Yankee trick. Many a business has been maintained on the crests of prosperity and respectability by associating it in the public mind with a church, a college, or an institution of charity. When Emerson religionized his literary agnosticism he was acting true to form. He was not so dreamy and unpractical as the shrewd Concord tradesmen believed. American history, past and present, bristles with illustrious instances of the success which awaits capable teachers of new religions. Emerson is a sublimated Mrs. Eddy.

It is interesting to watch him in action. He was a Pontifex Maximus, hedged about by awful ritual and ceremony. With stately and graceful gesture he gathered his toga about him—the same, doubtless, which appears in Daniel Chester French's statue—and floated away into the azure empyrean of transcendentalism with a blazing comet's tail of ardent souls in his wake. It is most magnificent charlatanry. He pontificates with gusto. He draws the curtains, lights the tapers, drapes the wall with symbolic tapestries, disposes the hourglasses, mattocks, skulls, and spades, most effectively, displays his crystal globes, and sprinkles a pinch of incense upon the smoldering tripod fires. In the mysterious and profound silence a voice is heard, the passionless level voice of a superterrestrial oracle: "Every soul is a celestial Venus to every other soul." The very abracadabra of magicians!

I do not deny to Emerson a certain high excellence that was rooted in austere virtues of character. But his virtues were more admirable than amiable. The reason is that they were mostly forms of a sensitive self-respect. His striking virtues were the qualities of a dominating defect, his towering pride. I almost doubt whether Emerson's virtues were virtues of character at all. "There are virtues of situation," says Chateaubriand, "which are too easily mistaken for general virtues, and which are merely local results." Emerson, the bold and brilliant insurgent, conformed thoroughly enough to the prim and subdued hues of his New England environment. He was a leading citizen of Concord, and eminently respectable. What a shock it would be to the neighbors if Mr. Emerson should get drunk, like that reprobate New Yorker, Edgar Allen Poe! or should mix with politicians, like that son of Agar, Daniel Webster! or waste his time fancifully discovering beauties in Romish countries and customs, like that strange, shy man, Nathaniel Hawthorne! or fail to understand the obvious spiritual advantages of clean clothes and a trim white dwelling amid green lawns, like that eccentric person, Henry David Thoreau! The simplicity, order, sobriety, and moral fervor, which constitute the chief excellence of Emerson and are the strong credentials of his loose thinking and his impudent self-esteem, were indigenous to the soil. Simplicity, order, sobriety, and moral fervor were the common New England prescriptions for securing an honorable and genteel position in the world. Emerson merely reflected in a faithful and splendid manner the prevalent virtues of the community in which his lines were laid. He never allowed his independence and self-reliance to get him into a scrape where the heavy hand of local disapproval might fall upon him.

Indeed, one of the amusing things about austere prophets like Emerson is the benignant way in which they permit themselves to be protected from the logical and unpleasant consequences of their asceticism. With a thrifty wife on guard, Tolstoy could afford to preach fanatically the holy doctrine of poverty. Emerson, who taught a proud aloofness from the petty affairs of making a living, submitted to be rescued by his less fine son-in-law from the toils of a crooked business agent. When Emerson's house was accidentally burned down, the apostle of self-reliance made shift to accept a substantial sum of money from sympathizing friends. One of them was Bancroft, to whom he sent the following letter of acknowledgment:

My dear and noble friend: I received three days ago the surprise of your letter and heroic gift. It requires more than gratitude—it requires somewhat heroic also to dare to receive it; for from such hands such a gift is a sort of crown, which might well make the recipient search himself for equal deserts. I cannot say that my seeking was quite satisfactory. Perhaps it lost itself still in saying—Did I not receive this Olympian gift from an Olympian? Well, I shall turn the order into coined money, and hold it subject to any claim of you and yours spoken or unspoken. I therefore here record that I have received from George Bancroft the sum of one thousand dollars which he is moved to send me on hearing of the burning of my house.

This letter has been admired by Emersonians. The graceful acceptance of a gift is a supreme triumph of good manners beyond the powers of a proud man.

The monumental self-complacency of Emerson was encouraged by the slavish adulation of his followers. Mr. Cabot tells a singular story about a certain meeting of the Saturday Club in honor of Shakespeare. Mr. Emerson had been invited to make a speech on the occasion. He rose from his chair, we read, "looked about him tranquilly for a minute or two, and then sat down, serene and unabashed, but unable to say a word upon a subject so familiar to his thoughts from boyhood." I hope the grin of some "Paddy" with a napkin on his arm saved the situation from becoming utterly unhuman. Emerson needed a setting of homage to feel at ease. He could not enjoy the company of men like Hawthorne and Thoreau, who met him on even terms. He took no pleasure in foreign travel, least of all in Latin countries whither the fame of the great Emerson had not penetrated. The rôle of seer and oracle was hard to sustain in common daylight and with matter-of-fact persons. Watch Emerson in the company of that plain man, Whittier, the Quaker poet:

"There lives an old Calvinist in that house, and she prays for me every day. I am glad she does. I pray for myself." "Does thee?" said Whittier. "What does thee pray for, friend Emerson?" "Well," replied Emerson, "when I first open my eyes upon the morning meadows, and look out upon the beautiful world, I thank God that I am alive, and that I live so near Boston."

At another time Emerson in Whittier's company expressed the opinion that the world had not yet seen the highest development of manhood. "Does thee think so?" said Whittier. "I suppose thee would admit that Jesus Christ is the highest development our world has seen." "Yes, yes, but not the highest it will see." "Does thee think the world has yet reached the ideals the Christ has set for mankind?" "No, no," said Emerson, "I think not." "Then is it not the part of wisdom to be content with what has been given us, till we have lived up to that ideal? And when we need something higher, Infinite Wisdom will supply our needs."

Emerson had a fastidious dislike of coming into close grips with the fundamental realities. Vagaries of thought like the theory of Divine immanence, and a turn for decking generalizations with jeweled phrases, are disturbed by pursuing the scrutiny of facts. It is possible to take Coleridge seriously, and Hazlitt seriously, and even Ruskin and Carlyle seriously. It requires no effort whatever to take Newman seriously. But we should never be tempted to take Emerson seriously. As a rhapsodist, however, he is a very entertaining writer.

RELIGION AND A CAREER: SIR JOHN DAY

ONE sometimes hears the complaint that Catholics are passed over in the distribution of secular honors and awards on account of their religion. Perhaps the complaint is not wholly without foundation. It can hardly be denied that irrelevant considerations, such as church affiliation and membership in secret societies, enter occasionally into the selection of men for distinguished posts, and in the recent past and, to some extent, in the present have borne with special severity upon Catholics. At the same time it is to be suspected that the complaint is often merely the excuse which mediocrity or inefficiency alleges for its failure, according to the common human practice of shifting our faults upon the shoulder of circumstance. In general, it may still be believed, merit will extort recognition from the most reluctant quarters. The world is looking for the man who can win its battles, run its business, and secure for it lucrative returns, irrespective of lodge or creed. No doubt, when qualifications are evenly balanced, religion is introduced here and there to turn the scale against the Catholic. This is unjust perhaps, but not discouraging. Genuine merit, after all, scorns dependence upon the lucky accidents and will have no rewards except those to which its claims are uncontested.

These reflections occurred to me while reading the pleasant biography of Sir John Day, written by one of his two Jesuit sons, and published some fifteen years ago. The subject of the biography was born in 1826 and died in 1908, after a brilliant career as an advocate and a judge. I select the following few items from the *Life* with the sole view of sketching very superficially the nature and extent of Sir John's success. He was born into an old Catholic family and received his education in Catholic schools, finishing his undergraduate studies in the Benedictine College at Downside. Admitted to the bar in 1849, three years after his marriage, and being in the enjoyment of a comfortable patrimony, he felt no urgency or inclination to practice his profession for several years. Some unfortunate speculations in mines, however, reduced him and his growing family to the verge of beggary and started him on his career. His beginnings were the usual beginnings of young lawyers without influential interests to pave the way to opportunity. During the unwelcome leisure of those early years he made a name for himself by editing a collection of parliamentary acts, known for many years as a legal classic, under the title of *Day's Common Law Procedure Acts*. About this time, too, he edited *Roscoe's Nisi Prius*, another well-known reference book among English lawyers. His practice in the meantime kept increasing, so that in 1880 his yearly income from fees exceeded sixty thousand dollars.

Sir John Day—in those years plain John Day—became one of the most brilliant and successful pleaders of the English bar. He owed his eminence to his great learning, industry, quick wit, skill in cross-examination, and his commanding power with judge and jury. It seems to have been the custom in England with eminent advocates to take young lawyers into their offices and train them in the ways of their calling. Some of the greatest legal lights in England were at one time among John Day's pupils. One of them, Judge Willis, after Day's death published *Recollections of Sir John Charles Frederick Day, for Nineteen Years Judge of the High Court.*

The honor of the High Court justiceship came in 1882. It is a post somewhat analogous to that of the Supreme Court of the United States. The salary of twenty-five thousand dollars, not half of his income as a lawyer, made the position less lucrative than honorable. In 1886 he was appointed chairman of the famous Belfast Riots Commission, and later on served with two other judges on the still more famous Parnell Commission. Judge Day was never very friendly to Irish aspirations, an attitude which his son surmises was due to a quarrel in Sir John's boyhood between the Irish and English students at Downside. His selection, therefore, as a commissioner in both cases was made over strong Irish protests. Still it would seem that Parnell and the Irish cause profited from the honesty and legal acumen of Judge Day. *The Dictionary of National Biography* is cited in proof that "it was Judge Day's insistence on early proof being tendered of the authenticity of the letters attributed to Parnell which forced Pigott into the box, and led to the collapse of that part of the case." When Sir John resigned from office in 1901 on account of his health and advanced years, *The Times* eulogized him and *The Morning Leader* printed the following humorous quatrain:

> Your judgments, My Lord, we could often admire,
>   Though they woke in the wicked dislike and dismay;
> But your very worst enemies, now you retire,
>   Will be ready to echo "Good Day!"

Judge Day survived his retirement seven years. When he died in 1908, his collection of modern pictures, selected and purchased by himself in the course of many years, brought at auction the very substantial sum of $517,730.

These facts leave no doubt that John Day was successful, as worldly success goes. Since his religion did not stand in the way, it is pertinent to inquire into the brand of Catholic religion which he practiced. His success would not be so very surprising if Judge Day were highly sensitive and reticent on the subject of his religious feelings and beliefs. The fact is that he was forceful and individualistic in his religious practices almost to the point of eccentricity. His son says that he never obtruded his religion upon the notice of others. This is very likely true. But on the other hand, it would be obviously misleading to assert that the judge's Catholic religion was of the timid sort. He was an

entirely fearless man who scorned concealments, and
the thoroughness which distinguished him as a great
jurist he carried into his religious life. "My personal
recollection of him," writes Cardinal Gasquet, "dates
back to the early fifties when as a boy I saw him as a
regular attendant at the Church of St. Mary of the
Angels, Bayswater, of which Monsignor Manning, the
future cardinal, had just become superior. I recall
today, although it is more than half a century ago, how
impressed we young people used to be by the earnestness which Sir John Day displayed whilst assisting at the
offices of the Church, and by his manifest and solid
piety. At that time he had been practicing at the bar for
some ten years, and was pointed out in London as a
young lawyer likely to become eminent in his profession. My boyish notions about gentlemen of the bar
were of the vaguest kind, but for some unknown reason
I did not associate an earnestness in the practice of religious duties with the profession. Possibly for that
very reason the sight of Mr. Day, as he then was,
throwing himself into it with obvious whole-hearted-
ness and sincerity and with the evident thoroughness of
entire belief, made an impression upon my mind which
remains fresh to this day." Going back still further in
his life we have the testimony of one of his preceptors
that "he was distinguished among his school fellows for
his morals, his piety toward God, and his reverence
toward his superiors."

This earnestness in his religious life characterized him through all the years of his prominence and success down to the very end. He hated slipshod habits in anything, but especially in religion. He always knelt bolt upright, and disliked to see people leaning back against the seat of the pew. "People will some day," he used to say in disgust, "take to lying down in church." He was accustomed to pass the time on railroad journeys saying his beads, and fellow passengers were treated to the spectacle of a distinguished personage unconsciously making quite a display of his rosary and moving his lips very energetically whilst he prayed. He had the scarcely laudable peculiarity of annoying those who were near him in church by the audible quality of his praying. "Once when staying in a country house," we are told, "where there was a private oratory, he was found quite unexpectedly by one of the other guests, also piously inclined, praying all alone in his most vehement manner. A lady once said of him that at times, when thus engaged, he appeared to be threatening the Almighty." The great lawyer could not understand the ways of shy apology in the practice of the Catholic faith. "It was always my father's practice," says his biographer, "to raise his hat when passing a Catholic church. One of his brother commissioners at Belfast noticed this, and by way of a joke—a poor and unworthy one—would nudge him as they passed other places of worship, with the result that Day saluted them, until he discovered that he was not being treated with good faith. His instinct for reverence and religious loyalty was deeply rooted."

The chapter on Judge Day's interior spirit is the most bracing portion of the book. His friend and memorialist, Judge Willis, tells how Day, although an experienced art critic, "would pass rapidly over any picture of too sensuous a character" in the continental art galleries which they visited together. He boldly refused to comply with precedent when, as a judge on circuit, he was expected to attend Anglican Sunday services in his official character. He heard Mass every morning and received Holy Communion weekly. In the Corpus Christi processions of his parish church he always carried the canopy, thus vividly reminding us of another bright luminary of the English bar, Blessed Thomas More. His parish priest and intimate friend, Canon Scannell, in addressing his congregation at the time of the judge's death, could say:

> Of his success at the bar, of his commanding presence on the bench of the High Courts of Justice, of his wisdom as a councilor of the king, the world will be speaking tomorrow. But it will not speak, for it is not its business to speak, of Sir John's daily attendance at Mass, whatever might be his work or the weather; of his weekly confession and Communion, of the time he gave to private prayer, of that interior life in which he looked through everything to God.

I am afraid I have not chosen the most interesting or the most significant features in the religious portrait of Sir John Day. Still I think it ought to be clear enough that his Catholic faith was not something to be secretly hoarded lest it interfere with his worldly success. He wore it proudly in the face of all men. And, strange as it may seem, it appears to have been a help rather than a hindrance on the road of secular preferment. His scrupulous fidelity and intense earnestness in the practice of his Catholic faith was of immense assistance to him in cultivating a stern sense of duty, indomitable courage, untiring industry, and a passionate attachment to truth and justice, admirable qualities which even a godless world includes among its most highly prized virtues. It is not the first and only time that piety has been the secret of worldly success; although, we confess, distinction and prosperity in this world do not come within the proper scope of piety, and, while constituting its severest test, are not its infallible accompaniments.

I have carefully scanned the life of Sir John Day to discover the secret of his unfailing piety from youth to old age throughout a most distracting career and in a world which blows cold from every quarter upon the supernatural life of a Catholic. I think I have discovered the secret in a single short paragraph of the biography. "He was a great reader of all thoughtful ascetical and theological literature. Longmans, Burns and Oates, and some other publishers must have loved him well." His evening reading always included a chapter from the New Testament in Greek. "A lifelong lover of the Psalmist, he, too, was determined to stave off the *sterilitas animæ meæ*." We are the easy victims of suggestion. If we allow the world the exclusive privilege of our little auditorium she will chain us to her chariot wheels. Sir John Day received and diligently cultivated the inestimable grace of knowing how to keep his mind and heart from becoming unstable and overbalanced by a foolishly single devotion to a purely human literature.

RELIGION AND A CAREER: LORD CHARLES RUSSELL

F EW men of the past generation afford better instances of the successful Catholic in the world of affairs than Lord Russell of Killowen, who died Lord Chief Justice of England in 1900. At the age of twenty-four, after some preliminary study and training in the law of his native Ireland, he went to London, and on the completion of a two-year course in English law was admitted to the English Bar. He found himself in a country not favorably disposed to his nationality and his religion, a poor man without friends or influential backing, newly married, and trusting in God and his own energy to establish a difficult footing in his overcrowded profession.

During 1859, his first year of practice, he earned five hundred dollars. He doubled his income every year for the first four years, until in 1869 it amounted to five thousand dollars. After that it continued to increase steadily, rising in the 70's to fifty thousand dollars, and in the 80's to ninety thousand dollars. In 1883 his fees amounted to $112,585. For two decades he figured as the leading advocate in the most famous cases tried in the courts of England, the most famous perhaps being the case of the forged letters of the *London Times*, in which he appeared for Parnell, and to the great satisfaction of Irishmen all over the world succeeded gloriously in teaching that haughty and arrogant newspaper a salutary lesson.

Lord Coleridge, Russell's predecessor in the Chief Justiceship, said of him while he was still practicing as an advocate, "He is the biggest advocate of the century." At the time of his death Sir George Lewis, the foremost of English solicitors, declared, "There never was a greater man at the English Bar than Russell." And shortly afterward Sir Richard Henn Collins, Lord Justice of Appeal, an authoritative representative of the English Bar, said in the course of a speech on Russell: "We are too near the open grave now to attempt to appreciate his relation to the great roll of distinguished advocates and distinguished judges who had filled the place that he filled. But of this I am quite sure, and in this I am certain the verdict of history will concur, that he was the most conspicuous forensic personality in the reign of Queen Victoria."

Eleven years later Mr. Asquith, addressing the English Parliament, had occasion to refer to the Parnell Commission, and mentioned Sir Charles Russell in these terms: "During nine months, never to be forgotten in my professional life, I sat behind the great advocate— I think the greatest advocate of our time."

Americans best remember Sir Charles Russell as the Attorney General in Gladstone's two Home Rule ministries. While he was holding that office he sustained the English claims at the arbitration conference in the dispute with the United States on the Bering Sea fisheries. Gladstone wished to make Russell Lord High Chancellor, and he strove vainly to repeal the law which excluded Catholics from that office. After Russell's elevation to the Chief Justiceship, in 1894, Gladstone wrote to him: "I have never got over my wrath at the failure of our effort to repeal the unjust and now ridiculous law which kept the highest office in your profession out of your reach. It is, however, some consolation to reflect that you are on a throne only a little less elevated, and very much more secure." Lord Russell's address on international law and arbitration at Saratoga Springs, in 1896, before the American Bar Association, was an event of importance to which the newspapers devoted large space. The following year he served as the principal arbiter on the British side in the Venezuelan arbitration, which met at Paris and settled a vexed question which had promised to involve England and the United States in war.

Enough has been said about Lord Russell's career to remove all doubts as to the completeness of his success. It remains to be seen whether in surroundings where his faith and nationality were highly unpopular he ever considered it necessary or advisable to practice economies and concealments in the one or the other. The first question which this line of thought suggests is, Why did he not remain in Ireland and give his country the benefit of his genius and industry? The answer to that question will throw a flood of light on contemporary Irish history and serve to explain the resolute action of the young Irishmen who, in more recent times, heroically waged an apparently hopeless fight for independence with the mightiest empire in the world.

When Russell went to England he was rapidly acquiring a rising reputation as a barrister in the north of Ireland. It seemed foolhardy to his friends and relations to abandon sure success at home for an experiment in a strange country where he would have to begin over again at the advanced age of twenty-seven. In a letter to Mrs. Mulholland, his wife's mother, he stated the reasons for his decisive step. He said that the English system of government in Ireland made it absolutely impossible for an Irishman to attain conspicuous success in public life and the legal profession without dishonest concessions in his dearest convictions as a Catholic and an Irishman. High office was used as a bribe to encourage coolness in faith and in national spirit. "Who are the men," he proceeds, "who have of late years risen, especially among the Catholics, to places that are reputed stations of honor and dignity? Men who rose because they forgot their early instincts which shot up like the young sapling unbent by the gardener's ligature, or who, if they didn't forget, then acted as if they did; men who did dirty business—excuse the speech— for the people in high places and so got their wages; men who, among their brethren, were not preëminent for learning and genius, but only remarkable for the yieldingness of their opinions; and so a profession which once reckoned great men in its ranks and stood marked for its independence would now be more fitly characterized for its servility and its absence of public virtue."

And so Charles Russell, like many another Irishman of genius and forceful character, was lost to his country. It is a striking commentary on the political condition of Ireland that he found in the early Victorian England, with all its violent prejudices against his race and his religion, a freer field for his ambition than in his Catholic native land. In our own day the bright young spirits of Ireland have elected to remain at home and to offer the sacrifice of their lives in order to liberate succeeding generations from the demoralizing influences of English rule. One of these high-minded and heroic young men has left us an expression of his sense of injustice. It is so similar in tone and language to that of Russell's that we can readily see that English rule in Ireland, though it might have improved in various details, was essentially the same old horrible incubus, as blighting to the best in Irish instinct and character as it had been seventy years ago. "No man," wrote the noble Terence MacSwiney, "must make peace till freedom is assured, for the moral plague that eats up a people whose independence is lost is more calamitous than any physical rending of limb from limb. Consider all the mean things and debasing tendencies that wither up a people in a state of slavery. There are the bribes of those in power to maintain their ascendency, the barter of every principle by timeservers, the corruption of public life and the apathy of private life, the hard struggle of those with high ideals, the conflict with all ignoble practices, the wearing down of patience, and in the end the quiet abandoning of the flag once bravely flourished; then the increased number of the apathetic and the general gloom, depression, and despair—everywhere a land decaying. Viciousness, meanness, cowardice, intolerance, every bad thing arises like a weed in the night and blights the land where freedom is dead; and the aspect of that land and the soul of that people become spectacles of disgust, revolting and terrible, terrible for the high things degraded and the great destinies imperiled."

In Ireland Charles Russell's most sacred convictions would have been regarded with official suspicion and discouragement; in England they might be looked upon with displeasure and disfavor. But young Russell was not seeking favor or preference. He trusted in his ability, industry, and force of character to break down popular prepossessions in any land of free institutions. He had sorrowfully left home and country rather than risk his fidelity to either, or submit to official temptations to moderate his religious beliefs, in the pursuit of a legitimate ambition. After that it was not likely that he would enter into weak compromises with his conscience for anything the world had to offer. Only once in his long career was anyone found to accuse him of temporizing. Some ten years after Russell had settled in England an unscrupulous political opponent for an Irish seat in Parliament made the accusation in the heat of a fiercely contested election. Russell's indignation might have been greater if the charge was not so obviously false. "To suggest to me in any form of words," he declared publicly, "that I was unwilling to be known in England as an Irishman or a Catholic is recklessly untrue and preposterously absurd." And great Irishmen of the time could bear him out. "He would not temporize," said Patrick MacMahon, "in the smallest way about his country or his religion to be made Lord Chancellor."

When we speak of Charles Russell's Catholic religion we must be understood as referring to a particularly intelligent and intense form of it. His religion was not what it so often happens to be in cases of distinguished success, little more than an hereditary appendage retained on some obscure principle of natural loyalty. Few men have enjoyed the spiritual advantages of his childhood and youth. There were five young Russells, and all of them entered the religious life except Charles. Their uncle was the celebrated Rev. Charles Russell, the friend of Newman and the president of Maynooth College, who wrote the classic life of Mezzofanti. The three girls of the family all became Sisters of Mercy. One of them, Sister Mary Baptist, is still remembered in San Francisco, where she founded houses of her order and was a prominent factor for nearly half a century in the growth of the city. The brother of

Charles entered the Society of Jesus and became the
gentle and charming publicist known far and wide in
Catholic circles as Father Matthew Russell.

One of the sisters, writing in 1899, has left us a pretty picture of their childhood days.

We were rather piously inclined all of us, and we had a little
association of our own and conferences on holy subjects. I remember the subject proposed in one of them by Kate was, What was
the best way to become a saint? And the unanimous opinion was
"to do our daily duties as well as ever we could, and to do all in
the presence of God to please Him"—a wise one surely, and containing as high spirituality as I, for my part, have ever learned since.
We had to read each day the Lives of the Saints in Alban Butler,
let them be long or short. It was no easy matter for four of us to
read some of the long ones in the leisure we had from other duties,
and I remember one day in particular when Charlie kept us such a
time looking for him, as he had our only book. About that time he
had been told always to ask if he did not understand what he was
reading. Being very obedient, and thus causing annoyance by constantly asking, he was next told to look out in the dictionary for
the meanings of the words. So this particular day, after a long
search, we found him in the carthouse, behind a cart tilted up,
with the Lives of the Saints and his dictionary.

In 1912 Father Russell wrote a book about his three
sisters. In its closing paragraph he says:

After telling so much about these beautiful souls, these three
Irish Sisters of Mercy, I am disposed to echo the historian's phrase
and to end by saying, "Such were the hearts that by prayer and sis-
terly sympathy were wound around the brave heart of Charles
Russell." In his boyhood their presence and their comradeship were
part of the training that helped to prepare him for his strenuous
fight with circumstances not always favorable for such success as
he was determined to achieve. From youth till age they followed

him with their love and gentle counsels and fervent prayers. In all the relations of life he showed himself the worthy brother of such sisters.

The close communion between the gifted members of this family endured to the end of their long lives despite separation and differences of employment. At the time of the Parnell Commission we find Sister Mary Baptist writing to Sir Charles in the following strain:

My DEAREST CHARLES: I need not tell you we are all watching with intense interest your struggle with the powers of the land, and glory in the success that seems to attend your efforts. Three things especially rejoice my heart: first, that you are true to your faith, then to your country and last to the principles of temperance. May God bless you, my dear brother, and preserve you ever true to these three points, and then your glory here will not lessen your glory hereafter. This is my prayer; for would I care for all the good you procure for the cause in which you are engaged if it deprived you of one degree of happiness hereafter? What doth it profit a man to gain the whole world if he suffer the loss of his own soul?

Some years before, Sister Mary Baptist, writing to a friend, said of her brother Charles:

So far, mixing with the world has not lessened his fidelity to his religious duties, thank God! But pray for him. He is only forty-nine this October, and he has ten children.

Happy the busy man of affairs whom such memories and associations keep in constant contact with the essential verities! Charles Russell had the grace to withstand any insidious encroachments of wealth and honors upon the vigor and robustness of his faith. When one of his daughters became a nun in 1900, the Lord Chief

Justice wrote to her: "We know you will do your duty, as it comes to you to do, well and thoroughly and unselfishly; and we have no fear that you will forget us. After all, it is something for us poor dusty creatures of the world, with our small selfish concerns and little ambitions, to have a stout young heart steadily praying for us." He never spoke of the dead without saying in a spirit of great devotion, "May God be merciful to his soul!" Even his worldly ambitions were inextricably woven with his faith. "My ambition," he said to a friend in 1883, "is to be the first Catholic Attorney General since the Reformation." It is pleasant to know that this ambition was fulfilled.

On his last circuit in Wales, and in the last month of his life, he startled the Sunday congregation in a little church where he had gone to hear Mass. One of the priests was without a server, and the Lord Chief Justice left his place in the church and acted as an acolyte, making the Latin responses devoutly and with familiar ease and distinctness. Ten days later he fell sick and was brought for medical attention to London, where he died after a surgical operation, August 10, 1900, at the age of sixty-eight. Several days before he had asked to see a priest, and made a general confession.

His last conscious moments are thus described by his biographers: "He requested the surgeon to prepare a diagram showing the nature of the operation. He looked over the diagram with Mr. Treves (the surgeon), asked many question, tapped the paper with his glass, as was his wont, and sought all the information that could be given to him. Afterward he expressed a wish to receive extreme unction before the operation was performed, and Father Basevi of the Oratory came and administered the last rites of the Church. The Chief asked Lady Russell to help him make the responses, saying he felt his voice very weak. But as a fact he answered clearly and distinctly; and when the priest told him to make an act of contrition, he began at once to say aloud the old familiar prayer which he had learned at his mother's knee, 'O my God, I am heartily sorry that I have offended Thee, and I detest my sins most sincerely because they are displeasing to Thee.' "

How did Charles Russell's religion affect his life and conduct on the broad arena of public affairs? Fortunately, we have the testimony of a disinterested man of the world, who was not a Catholic and who speaks, as it were, from the outside. In an article which appeared in the *Fortnightly* soon after Lord Russell's death, Mr. Edward Dicey, one of the foremost political writers of the day, summed up his impressions of a long friendship in the following words: "One result of his religious training should be fairly noted. He was a man whose life had been passed among men of the world, belonging as a rule to a class among whom a certain freedom of language is habitual. Yet without any pretense of setting up a higher standard of morality than his associates, his conversation was at all times exceptionally free from offence. In as far as my observation went, the sort of stories told in club smoking rooms and at bar messes always met with a reception from Russell which did not encourage their repetition; and, though he was by no means squeamish in his language, he carefully avoided all talk which even lay on the borderland of impropriety. In the course of a chequered life I have known many men whose conversation was void of offence, but then they were not, as a rule, men who had lived in the society in which Russell by the exigencies of his position and by his tastes had necessarily passed the greater part of his life. I always attributed his distaste for loose conversation of any kind to the influence of religion, which had taken a strong hold of his mind from the days of his early education. I was the more impressed by this peculiarity from the fact that Russell was so emphatically a man with all the tastes, ideas, convictions, and prejudices of a strong, vigorous, manly nature, and with nothing of femininity about him unless it were an almost womanly kindness of heart."

It was thus that Charles Russell allowed the beauty and strength of his faith to shine through his life. He recked not whether the world would like it or not. As a matter of fact, the world was constrained to admire what it saw. If all Catholic men carried into public life the same fearless fidelity to their faith that characterized Lord Russell of Killowen, a world which judges everything by such fruits as it can see might have less difficulty in discovering the City on the Hill. And while public life would undoubtedly benefit by the presence

of such high-minded and sterling Catholics, they themselves would perhaps be astonished to learn that their
trueness to their religion was more of a help than a
hindrance in all proud and honest achievement.

A POET OF OUR LADY

ABOUT three miles outside the city of Limerick, on a road which is the prolongation of O'Connell Street, stands the Jesuit college of Mungret. Many American priests, and several members of the American hierarchy, have received their classical education there. It stands on a slight rise, well back from the road, in spacious grounds, and is approached by a long, old-world avenue laid on the greenest of green grass, and bordered by stately trees. The plain severity of the architectural lines gives the buildings a suggestion of gaunt purpose, perhaps not out of character in an institution which is tremendously in earnest and sends every year messengers of peace to all the ends of the earth. There is a plain simplicity, too, in the natural setting of the college—low-lying, open country breaking at the horizon into high heather-topped hills. In front, some four or five miles across flat meadows and pastures, rise the hills of Clare; and, somewhere in the middle distance, the "noble Shannon" flows down to the sea. The river is not visible from the college except during spring floods; and it is rather startling to watch great ships from America and Japan that appear to be gliding across the level fields to the docks of Limerick.

When I visited the college in the summer of 1924, I came on the traces, it seems to me, of a rather remarkable man, a Marian poet whose unurged claims to Catholic attention should not be allowed to pass unheeded. In the preceding January, Father Francis Shaw, on the teaching staff of the college, had died in a Dublin hospital. His associates whom I met were eager to talk about him, about his many lovable qualities, his whimsical humor, his gallantry in the face of suffering, his quiet strength, and his work—not the routine work of college life, which he performed well, but underground work carried on beneath the traffic of life so skilfully as to remain hidden until his death. They showed me his manuscript papers, filled with patristic erudition on devotion to Our Lady, original meditations and studies on the same subject, and finally a sonnet sequence in which the smoldering fires of long thought and prayer leap into flame. It was a rather thrilling experience. The Clare hills made an undulating outline on the window where I sat; and it seemed to me, as I read these sonnets in an old notebook, that I was very close to the soul of Ireland.

There were thirty-four sonnets in all. Before I quote from them I shall give a brief account of their writer. Francis Shaw was born in 1881. He lost his parents at an early age, and was placed under the guardianship of a relation, the Right Reverend Dr. Fogarty, the Bishop of Killaloe. After his classical studies in Castleknock College, he went to Newcastle-on-Tyne to study en-

gineering. In new and strongly Protestant surroundings, he found himself obliged to defend his religion
among casual companions; and he had recourse to some
Jesuits in the matter of polishing up his armor and con-
ditioning his controversial weapons. The incident ended
in his entering the Jesuit novitiate of the Irish Province.
When he had completed his Jesuit course, the Great
War was on. Father Shaw immediately offered his
services as an army chaplain and served in France, India,
East Africa, and Mesopotamia, until 1919. He went
to Mungret the following year.

Father Shaw's health began to fail during his first
year in the army; but nothing serious was anticipated,
probably because he was a renowned athlete, famous in
Ireland and in the army for his prowess in cricket and
football. The story is still told of how he kicked the
winning goal for his regiment with an ankle so badly in-
jured that it kept him in bed for six weeks after the
game. It was only when he went to the hospital a few
months before the end that medical science pronounced
his case hopeless. But he had long suspected the truth
and used to make it the subject of jests. As we shall
see in two of his sonnets, his light-heartedness in the
shadow of doom was not a reckless pose, but rather that
keen sense of the humor of life which a strong hold on
the eternal things has often been known to impart.

Writing from a sick bed in a Bagdad hospital to an
American friend in Bombay, he began his letter,

Here lies poor Shaw
On this lone bed,
Not buried yet
Because not dead.

During his last days he would remain patiently in an uncomfortable position to avoid troubling his nurse.

As a master, first at Clongowes and afterward at Mungret, he was always popular with the students. His skill in athletics doubtless helped. But they also tell you that it was a quiet and gentle courtesy which won the boys while imposing restraint. One catches the hint of a subtle aloofness in the pictures that emerge from affectionate talk about him. He was always good company, fertile and resourceful in a dull hour; but he had the capacity of enjoying solitude. The conventional busy ant, seeing him moving aimlessly over the meadows or watching the stars, might have concluded that he could be better employed in the enterprise of improving each shining moment. But it happened to be no idle mooning. Father Shaw was intent upon increasing his secret store while the day lasted.

It is not wholly fair to make selections from a sequence in which the most striking effect is cumulative, where every single stone contributes to the final impression. The sonnets are Shakespearean in structure, and curiously Shakespearean in their accommodation of the grand style to the serious expression of a personal experience. The extravagances of Elizabethan usage among poets cease to be such on a theme like Father Shaw's. The sonneteer of Our Lady need not appeal to poetic conventions to justify high-sounding phrases and daring invention. The manner of Shakespeare's famous sonnets is almost absurdly above the subject. Father Shaw's employment of it in the service of her, who is the pinnacle of created perfection, produces a satisfying sense of fitness.

What Catholic teacher of youth, in despair of the miracles of genius, has not found support in the following thought?

> Oh, I could live in envy of that band
>   Of chosen spirits, whose power it is to waken
> Young love to beauty, who with magic hand
>   Have from the very founts of Heaven taken
> Colors to blend on earth, or with sweet words
>   Woven high fancies to subdue the mind,
> Or who have spun of simple sounds such chords
>   As sorrow, love, and victory unbind
> Within the listening soul. Oh, I could fret,
>   These envying their high prerogative,
> But that the Providence, which theirs did set,
>   Also to me a glorious task doth give—
> To wed young love to Beauty, not by arts,
>   But sowing love of thee in youthful hearts.

Not the least of the attraction of these sonnets are the passing glimpses, exciting curiosity rather than satisfying it, into the recesses of the writer's life. Perhaps no one knows the tragedy to which there is allusion here:

High into space I raised my castle towers,
  Gleaming with glory in the summer air.
All one short year I spent the glowing hours
  A-building, till the walls were grown so fair
Sweet joy came there to live. The single thought
  Of this my castle soaring to the skies
Kept a whole autumn beautiful, and brought
  Sunshine to winter, and filled up the eyes
Of the young spring with an unwonted grace,
  And drew the summer to a magic birth.
Today when the last stone was set in place,
  My castle sank in ruins to the earth.
Teach me, wise Mother of a Son most wise,
  Only thy Son to love, all else despise.

And only one who liked to walk alone across meadows and under stars could write:

Last night across the sky I watched Orion
  Move in his glittering state, his bright sword gleaming;
Behind him Sirius; then the pawing Lion
  From his dark lair, his mane with jewels streaming.
I saw the Virgin near the Serpent walking,
  And southward Spica's fairy sail outspread,
And that great boor, Arcturus, westward stalking,
  And low on the horizon, in his head
A ruby shining, Scorpius: then the flame
  Of Vega burned, and Pegasus outtrod
Before the Charioteer. "The heavens proclaim."
  I cried in ecstasy, "the glory of God."
Yet not the heavens in all their splendor dressed,
  As much as only thou, Him manifest.

Father Shaw knew he was rifling a chest of rare music
when he chose these starry names. He laid botany
under contribution as well:

The high hills ranged, the sparkling streams that fall,
    The sea, the sky, the precious flowers that throw,
To bind the earth in the sun's fruitful thrall,
    Across brown meadows chains of gold and snow,
Hawkweeds and hawkbits, picrises, and snatches
    Of meadow daisies in the soft wind stirring,
The slender vetch, and the blue jewelled patches
    Of dark-eyed speedwell, with a sense unerring
Of common nature I have surely chosen
    Unfailing comrades of this earth probation,
In summer always near, and in the frozen
    Harsh winter's reign, near in imagination.
Yet how unbearable were life, and lonely,
    If without thee I had these others only!

In some of the sonnets, ardor burns into a white glow which is rather startling:

If from this ebon sky the pale moon, hurled,
    Should glide through starlit vacancy to doom
Below the great round shoulder of the world,
    Who would build so bright a sunshine for the gloom?
Or who, amid the swoon of hot July,
    If her red roses, struck with pestilent breath,
Dissolved, could frame again the season's high
    Magnificence before the roses' death?
Thou art the stainless moon, from thee out-thrown
    The dazzling splendors of the Invisible Light
Flood the dim world; thou art the Rose fresh-blown
    Whose beauty chains His Beauty to my sight.
God had been less our God to us if He
    Had come direct from heaven, nor thought of thee.

The modern ear, trained to preciosity of epithet, may find fault with some of the easy and obvious phrases in these sonnets. But it is to be remembered that the essence of poetry does not consist in verbal felicities. Else Robert Burns, for an instance, would have to be excluded from the realms of gold. The fashion of poetry is not identical with its substance. If the soul shines through the medium, it is what we especially require: that phenomenon alone serves notice that the art is there whether we recognize it as contemporary or not. And it seems to me that in these thirty-four sonnets the soul of Father Shaw animates them with its own vital warmth. They would be mere human documents if the author of them had not triumphed over the supreme difficulty of translating piercing personal experience into the universal formula of art. Preciosity did not exist yesterday, and will probably not exist tomorrow, and hence cannot be said to enter into the formula of poetry.

The last two sonnets in the sequence were written after Father Shaw had learned the truth that the rest of his life on earth was to be a slow and painful dying. In the worn old notebook these two sonnets were written, as none of the others were, in bright-red ink. That they are not painful reading is, I submit, a strong proof that the art employed in writing them was of no mean order. They carry a noble series of meditative poems to an intensely dramatic culmination of praise and triumph.

> All gifts of preciousness I love, I took
>   In thy Son's world, and gave to thee; thine eyes
> Have watched them numbered in the heavenly Book—
>   Gifts that a Queen of Heaven may not despise.

I gave thee the blue summer, the dark hills,
   And meadows ripening in the sultry haze,
The sea, the flowered plains, and what else fills
   The earth with loveliness. I gave thee praise
In song and speech. But ever in my soul
   Thy voice keeps urging, not yet satisfied.
"What now remains?" I cry, "Have I not whole
   Creations given? What have I yet denied?"
"One gift," thy answer, "all these gifts above,
   You still deny me, giving not your love."

The veil is rent, so deftly woven; and I
   That would not see—in false complacence living,
Myself deceived—surrender the great lie,
   That love is love that lives by easy giving.
Abashed I front the dire acknowledgment
   That my rich offerings carried to thy shrine
Were but the vassal coins of sentiment,
   Less careful of thy worship than of mine.
Giftless I stand. Be merciful, great Queen,
   Till I grow strong to offer gifts of price,
Not summer skies, hills, oceans, fields of green,
   But trifles dipped in blood of Sacrifice;
That, when thine eye scans my new gifts above,
   Thy voice proclaim, "Lo! here are gifts of love."

Father Shaw was no academic experimenter in verse. His sonnets indicate long practice and considerable facility in verse-writing; but I was informed, if my memory is not deceiving me, that he never appeared in print as a poet before the publication of some of the sonnets over a pseudonym in the *Mungret Annual*. A copy was sent to a sister in London, shortly after Father Shaw's death, and she wrote to one of his colleagues, expressing genuine surprise at the discovery that her brother Frank, with whom she was in constant communication, had so successfully concealed his gift from her.

The reticence is not wholly unintelligible. There was something beautifully medieval in Father Shaw's mood, something of the spirit of chivalry, and the crusades, and the building of cathedrals to our Blessed Mother, in which achievement was more a prayer than a triumph of skill. Father Shaw's sonnet-writing was too intricately woven with his devotion to be regarded as material for display. It had much of the character of a private piety, a real intimacy, too fine for coarse advertisement, between him and his heavenly Mother.